RETIREMENT PLANNING GUIDE FOR SINGLE WOMEN

Create Your Ideal Life and Secure Your Future

Hector Victory Vivian

Table of Contents

INTRODUCTION

Why Retirement Planning Is Essential for Single Women

Retirement planning is an essential step for anyone, but for single women, it takes on a unique level of importance. Unlike individuals who may have a partner to share financial responsibilities or fallback support, single women often bear the full weight of ensuring their own financial security. This reality makes it even more critical to develop a clear and sustainable plan for retirement.

Single women face unique challenges that require thoughtful preparation. For instance, women generally live longer than men, meaning they will need to stretch their savings over a longer period. Additionally, gender pay gaps throughout a woman's career can result in lower lifetime earnings and, consequently, smaller retirement savings.

These factors underscore the importance of starting early and planning strategically to close any potential financial gaps.

Financial independence is another key factor. Retirement planning empowers single women to maintain control over their lives, even after they leave the workforce. A well-prepared retirement plan ensures that a woman can continue to live on her own terms without relying on family, friends, or external assistance. This independence is not only about money but also about the freedom to make choices that align with her values and lifestyle preferences.

A critical aspect of planning is understanding the cost of healthcare, which tends to rise significantly in later years. As we age, medical expenses become a substantial part of our budgets. Having a robust financial plan that accounts for these costs provides peace of mind and allows single women to access the care they need without financial strain.

Additionally, retirement is not just about securing finances; it's about creating a fulfilling and enjoyable phase of life. Many single women view retirement as an opportunity to explore hobbies, travel, volunteer, or even start new ventures. These pursuits often require careful budgeting to ensure funds are available for both necessities and aspirations.

For single women, the absence of a spouse or partner means that their retirement plan must be self-reliant and resilient to potential risks, such as unexpected expenses or market fluctuations. This requires a proactive approach to building savings, diversifying investments, and setting up safety nets like insurance and emergency funds.

Retirement planning also involves more than just saving money. It requires setting clear goals and aligning them with a realistic timeline. For example, understanding when to start saving, how much to contribute, and where to invest are critical decisions that shape a woman's financial future. Furthermore, tools like retirement accounts, employer-sponsored plans, and social security benefits can all play vital roles in achieving a secure retirement.

Retirement planning for single women is about creating a roadmap for a life that is both secure and fulfilling. It is an opportunity to take charge of one's future, overcome challenges, and embrace the possibility of a rewarding retirement. By planning thoughtfully, single women can ensure they are prepared to meet the financial and lifestyle demands of their golden years while enjoying the freedom and independence they have worked hard to achieve.

CHAPTER 1

Assessing Your Financial Situation

Understanding Your Current Financial Landscape

Understanding your current financial landscape is the first and most critical step in creating a successful retirement plan. For single women, this process means taking a clear and honest look at where you stand financially today. This foundation provides the necessary insights to make informed decisions about the future and ensures that your retirement goals align with your present situation.

To begin, it's essential to define what a financial landscape includes. It consists of four main components: assets, liabilities, income, and expenses. These elements work together to form a complete picture of your financial health. Analyzing each of them will help you identify areas where you are doing well and areas that may need improvement.

Assets represent the things you own that have financial value. These can include savings accounts, retirement accounts like a 401(k) or IRA, real estate, vehicles, and investments such as stocks or mutual funds. Even smaller assets, like valuable jewelry or collectibles, count. Take time to make a list of all your assets and note their current value. It's also helpful to separate your assets into liquid (easily converted into cash, like savings accounts) and non-liquid (less accessible, like property). This will give you a clear idea of what resources you have readily available and what might require time or effort to use.

Liabilities are the opposite of assets; they represent what you owe. Common liabilities include credit card debt, student loans, car loans, and mortgages.

Just like with assets, make a list of all your liabilities, noting the total amount owed, interest rates, and monthly payment amounts. By understanding your liabilities, you can see how much of your monthly income is tied up in debt and identify areas to reduce these obligations.

Income is another crucial part of your financial picture. It includes your earnings from work, side hustles, or freelance projects. If you receive income from other sources, such as rental properties or investments, be sure to include those as well. The goal here is to understand how much money you have coming in each month and how stable that income is. For example, income from a salaried job may be more predictable than income from freelance work, which can fluctuate.

Expenses are the final piece of the puzzle. These are the costs of your day-to-day life, including housing, utilities, groceries, transportation, insurance, and other bills. Expenses can also include discretionary spending, such as dining out, travel, or entertainment. Tracking your expenses over a few months will give you a realistic picture of where your money goes. Many people find it helpful to categorize their expenses into "needs" and "wants." This can make it easier to identify areas where you might be able to cut back if needed.

Once you've gathered this information, it's time to analyze it. Start by calculating your **net worth**, which is simply the total value of your assets minus your liabilities. A positive net worth means you own more than you owe, while a negative net worth indicates the opposite. This number is a snapshot of your overall financial health and can serve as a baseline to measure your progress over time.

Next, look at your cash flow, which is the difference between your monthly income and expenses. A positive cash flow means you're living within your means and potentially saving money, while a negative cash flow indicates that you're spending more than you earn. Understanding your cash flow is critical for identifying areas where you can save more for retirement or pay down debt.

Debt management is another important area to focus on. High-interest debt, like credit card balances, can quickly eat away at your resources. If you have multiple debts, consider using strategies like the debt snowball method, which involves paying off smaller debts first, or the debt avalanche method, which prioritizes debts with the highest interest rates. Reducing debt not only improves your financial health but also frees up more money to invest in your retirement future.

Saving for retirement should also be a top priority. If you haven't already, take advantage of retirement accounts such as a 401(k) if your employer offers one, especially if they provide matching contributions. This is essentially free money that can significantly boost your savings over time. If a 401(k) isn't available, consider opening an individual retirement account (IRA). Both options offer tax advantages that can help your money grow faster.

Additionally, it's essential to have an emergency fund. This is a savings account with enough money to cover three to six months of living expenses in case of unexpected events, like job loss or medical emergencies. Having an emergency fund ensures that you won't have to dip into your retirement savings when life throws you a curveball.

Another key aspect of assessing your financial situation is identifying areas where you might be able to increase your income or reduce your expenses. For example, could you take on a part-time job or freelance work to boost your earnings? Are there subscriptions or memberships you're not using that you could cancel? Small changes can add up over time, creating more room in your budget for savings.

Once you've completed your financial assessment, it's important to revisit it regularly. Life circumstances change; jobs, health, and even goals can shift over time. By periodically reviewing your financial landscape, you can make adjustments as needed to stay on track.

Understanding your financial landscape is the foundation of effective retirement planning. By taking stock of your assets, liabilities, income, and expenses, you gain a clear understanding of where you stand today. This knowledge empowers you to make informed decisions about your future, prioritize your goals, and create a roadmap that leads to a secure and fulfilling retirement. It's not just about the numbers; it's about building a life of financial independence and peace of mind.

Calculating Retirement Needs Based on Your Lifestyle

Calculating how much money you will need for retirement is one of the most critical steps in planning for the future. This calculation requires careful thought about your lifestyle, life expectancy, and the impact of inflation over time. By understanding these factors, you can estimate your retirement savings needs and create a plan that aligns with your goals and dreams.

Your personal lifestyle preference play a significant role in determining how much money you will need during retirement. Think about the type of life you envision. Do you plan to travel extensively, pursue hobbies, or relocate to a different city? Perhaps you prefer a simpler, quieter life, focusing on spending time with family, volunteering, or enjoying local activities. Your lifestyle choices will directly influence your retirement expenses, as they dictate how much you will need to cover daily living costs, leisure activities, and other priorities.

To estimate your retirement lifestyle costs, start by calculating your current living expenses. Include housing, utilities, transportation, food, healthcare, insurance, and other recurring bills. Next, consider how these expenses might change in retirement. For example, you might save money on work-related costs such as commuting or professional attire, but you may also face higher healthcare expenses or additional spending on hobbies and travel. If you plan to downsize your home, relocate to a more affordable area, or eliminate debt before retiring, factor those adjustments into your calculations.

Inflation is another critical factor to account for when calculating retirement needs. Over time, the cost of goods and services tends to rise, which means your money will not have the same purchasing power in the future as it does today. For example, the cost of healthcare, which is already a significant expense in retirement, is expected to increase at a higher rate than general inflation. To ensure your savings keep up with inflation, it's essential to include a buffer in your calculations. Many financial planners recommend using an average inflation rate of 2% to 3% per year when estimating future costs.

Once you've considered these factors, you can begin to calculate your retirement savings needs. A common guideline is the 80% rule, which suggests that you will need approximately 80% of your pre-retirement income to maintain your standard of living in retirement. For example, if you earn $50,000 annually before retirement, you might need $40,000 per year during retirement. However, this percentage can vary based on your lifestyle and plans. If you anticipate higher expenses due to travel, healthcare, or other factors, you may need closer to 100% of your pre-retirement income.

Another useful approach is to calculate your total retirement savings goal by multiplying your estimated annual retirement expenses by the number of years you expect to be retired. For instance, if you estimate needing $40,000 per year and plan for a 25-year retirement, your total savings goal would be $1 million. This method provides a straightforward way to determine how much you need to save in total.

It's also important to factor in other sources of income, such as Social Security benefits, pensions, or annuities. These income streams can reduce the amount you need to save. However, keep in mind that relying solely on Social Security is not recommended, as it is designed to supplement retirement savings rather than fully replace pre-retirement income. To estimate your Social Security benefits, you can use online calculators or request a statement from the Social Security Administration.

Another consideration is your investment strategy. The way your money is invested will impact how much it grows over time. For example, younger individuals may choose a more aggressive investment strategy with higher-risk, higher-reward options, while those nearing retirement might shift to safer, more stable investments. The rate of return on your investments will affect how much you need to save each year to reach your goal.

It's essential to revisit your calculations periodically, as circumstances and financial markets can change. For example, unexpected health issues, changes in the economy, or adjustments to your retirement goals may require you to revise your savings target. Regularly updating your plan ensures that you remain on track and prepared for any changes that come your way.

Building a retirement budget can help you manage your savings effectively. By estimating your retirement income and expenses, you can create a clear roadmap for how your money will be spent. This budget should include both fixed expenses, such as housing and healthcare, and discretionary expenses, such as travel and entertainment. Having a detailed budget allows you to prioritize your spending and ensure that your savings are used wisely.

Estimating retirement savings needs is a comprehensive process that involves analyzing your lifestyle preferences and accounting for inflation. By carefully considering these factors and using tools such as the 80% rule and retirement budget, you can calculate a savings target that aligns with your goals. This proactive approach not only helps you prepare for a secure financial future but also provides peace of mind as you work toward achieving your dream retirement.

Evaluating Debt and Creating a Plan to Eliminate It

Evaluating and eliminating debt is a crucial step in building a strong retirement plan. Debt can significantly impact your ability to save, invest, and achieve financial independence. For single women, the challenge is even more pressing, as there may not be a partner's income to help share the financial burden. By addressing debt early and systematically, you can free up resources for retirement savings and enjoy greater peace of mind.

The first step in tackling debt is to identify all your outstanding obligations. Start by gathering all the information about your debts, including credit cards, student loans, personal loans, car loans, and mortgages. For each debt, note the total amount owed, interest rate, minimum monthly payment, and due date. Creating a detailed list or spreadsheet will give you a clear picture of what you owe and to whom. This information is essential for understanding your current financial position and prioritizing which debts to address first.

Once you have a complete list of your debts, the next step is to evaluate their impact on your finances. High-interest debts, such as credit cards, can be particularly harmful because they grow quickly over time. These debts should take priority in your repayment plan. Low-interest debts, such as mortgages or federal student loans, may be less urgent, but they still need to be managed effectively to avoid long-term strain on your finances.

To eliminate debt, start by choosing a repayment strategy that aligns with your goals and financial situation. Two popular methods are the debt snowball and the debt avalanche.

The debt snowball method involves paying off your smallest debts first while making minimum payments on larger ones. As each small debt is eliminated, you redirect the freed-up money to the next smallest debt, creating momentum and a sense of accomplishment. This approach is ideal for those who need motivation to stay on track.

- The debt avalanche method focuses on paying off debts with the highest interest rates first. By targeting high-interest debts, you save more money over time, as you reduce the amount of interest you pay. This method is best for those who want to minimize the overall cost of their debt.

Whichever method you choose, it's important to prioritize consistent payments. Set up automatic payments or reminders to ensure you never miss a due date, as late fees and penalties can add to your debt burden. Consistency is key to making progress, even if the steps feel small at first.

If your budget is tight, consider finding ways to increase your income or reduce expenses to free up more money for debt repayment. Taking on a part-time job, selling unused items, or starting a side hustle can provide extra cash to put toward your debts. At the same time, review your monthly expenses for areas where you can cut back. For example, dining out less often, canceling unused subscriptions, or shopping for better insurance rates can make a noticeable difference.

Another effective strategy is to negotiate with creditors. If you're struggling to make payments, reach out to your lenders to discuss options such as lower interest rates, reduced payments, or extended repayment terms. Many creditors are willing to work with borrowers who demonstrate a commitment to repaying their debts. In some cases, consolidating debts into a single loan with a lower interest rate can simplify repayment and save money.

For those with significant debt, credit counseling services can be a valuable resource. Credit counselors are financial professionals who can help you develop a personalized debt management plan. They may also negotiate with creditors on your behalf to secure better terms. Be sure to choose a reputable counseling agency, preferably one accredited by organizations such as the National Foundation for Credit Counseling.

As you work to eliminate debt, it's important to avoid taking on new debts. This means resisting the temptation to use credit cards for unnecessary purchases or taking out loans for non-essential expenses. Building a habit of living within your means is crucial for staying debt-free and maintaining financial stability.

In addition to eliminating existing debt, it's wise to establish an emergency fund. This is a savings account with enough money to cover three to six months of living expenses. An emergency fund acts as a financial safety net, preventing you from relying on credit cards or loans in the event of unexpected expenses, such as medical bills or car repairs. By having this buffer, you reduce the likelihood of falling back into debt.

Tracking your progress is another essential part of staying motivated. Regularly review your repayment plan to see how much progress you've made and adjust your strategy as needed. Celebrate small victories, such as paying off a credit card or reducing a loan balance, as these milestones reinforce your commitment to becoming debt-free.

Remember that eliminating debt is not just about numbers; it's about creating a foundation for a secure and fulfilling retirement. Every dollar you pay off brings you closer to financial independence and gives you more freedom to focus on saving for the future. By addressing debt head-on and maintaining discipline, you empower yourself to take control of your finances and achieve your retirement goals.

Evaluating and eliminating debt requires a systematic approach that starts with understanding what you owe and creating a clear repayment plan. By choosing the right strategy, staying consistent, and avoiding new debts, you can reduce your financial burden and free up resources for retirement. This proactive approach not only strengthens your financial position but also gives

you confidence and peace of mind as you prepare
for the next chapter of your life.

CHAPTER 2

Building a Strong Financial Foundation

Setting Financial Goals for Retirement

Setting realistic financial goals for retirement is essential to creating a roadmap that ensures a secure and fulfilling future. These goals act as a compass, guiding your financial decisions and helping you prioritize how to save, invest, and spend. For single women, having a clear plan is even more critical as they often need to independently manage their retirement needs. Goals should be specific, measurable, and tailored to fit your unique lifestyle and aspirations.

To begin, it's important to distinguish between short-term and long-term financial goals. Both are necessary components of a solid retirement plan, but they serve different purposes. Short-term goals are focused on immediate actions and milestones that build the foundation for long-term success. Long-term goals, on the other hand, focus on the ultimate outcome; retirement itself.

Short-term goals typically cover a time frame of one to five years and are crucial for establishing financial stability. Examples of short-term goals include creating an emergency fund, paying off high-interest debt, or increasing retirement contributions. These goals help you lay the groundwork for financial security, ensuring that you can handle unexpected expenses and save consistently without interruptions. For instance, if you don't already have an emergency fund, setting a goal to save three to six months' worth of living expenses within two years can provide peace of mind and prevent setbacks.

Another short-term goal might be to maximize contributions to your retirement accounts, such as a 401(k) or an individual retirement account (IRA). Many employers offer matching contributions for 401(k) plans, which is essentially free money. If you aren't already contributing enough to get the full match, setting a goal to increase your contributions gradually over the next few years can make a significant difference in your retirement savings. This step ensures you're taking full advantage of available resources while building a habit of consistent saving.

Long-term goals, on the other hand, focus on what you want your retirement to look like. These goals require careful consideration of your desired lifestyle, expected retirement age, and the amount of money needed to sustain that lifestyle. For example, you might have a long-term goal of retiring at age 65 with $1.5 million in savings. This number can be based on a combination of factors, including your current income, estimated future expenses, and how long you expect to live in retirement.

When setting long-term goals, it's essential to consider specific financial needs for retirement. These include housing, healthcare, daily living expenses, and discretionary spending on activities such as travel, hobbies, or supporting loved ones. Think about whether you plan to stay in your current home, downsize, or move to a new location. Each scenario comes with different costs that should be factored into your goals.

Inflation is another critical factor in long-term planning. Over time, the cost of goods and services rises, meaning your money will need to stretch further in the future. For example, healthcare expenses tend to increase faster than general inflation and are a significant concern for retirees. Setting a financial goal that accounts for inflation ensures that your retirement savings retain their purchasing power.

Once you've identified your short-term and long-term goals, it's important to make them specific and measurable. Vague goals like "save for retirement" are not actionable. Instead, break your goals down into clear, achievable steps. For example, rather than simply aiming to "save more," set a specific goal to save $500 per month for the next five years or to increase your retirement account contributions by 1% each year.

Next, prioritize your goals based on urgency and impact. Short-term goals, such as eliminating debt or creating an emergency fund, often take precedence because they provide the foundation for pursuing long-term goals. Once these immediate needs are addressed, you can shift your focus to larger, long-term objectives. This prioritization ensures that your financial plan remains balanced and realistic.

It's also essential to regularly review and adjust your goals. Life circumstances can change unexpectedly, whether due to a new job, health issues, or shifts in your personal priorities. Periodically reassessing your goals allows you to stay on track and make adjustments as needed. For example, if you receive a significant raise, you might decide to increase your retirement contributions or set new goals for discretionary spending.

One helpful tool for staying focused on your goals is the SMART framework. This approach ensures that goals are Specific, Measurable, Achievable, Relevant, and Time-bound. For instance, instead of saying, "I want to save for healthcare expenses," a SMART goal might be, "I will save $10,000 in a health savings account within five years to cover future medical costs." This level of clarity makes it easier to track progress and remain committed.

Another critical element of goal-setting is aligning your actions with your values and priorities. For single women, retirement planning might involve not just securing financial independence but also leaving a legacy, supporting family members, or contributing to causes they care about. Reflecting on what matters most to you can help ensure that your financial goals align with your personal values, making the process more meaningful and motivating.

Don't forget to celebrate milestones along the way. Achieving financial goals, whether short-term or long-term, requires discipline and effort. Recognizing your progress reinforces positive habits and encourages you to stay committed. For example, when you pay off a credit card or reach a savings milestone, treat yourself to a small reward that doesn't derail your financial plan.

Setting realistic financial goals for retirement involves a combination of short-term actions and long-term planning. By identifying clear, specific objectives and prioritizing them based on your needs and aspirations, you can create a roadmap that leads to financial security and independence. Regularly reviewing and adjusting your goals ensures they remain relevant and achievable, empowering you to build a strong foundation for a comfortable and fulfilling retirement.

Establishing an Emergency Fund

An emergency fund is one of the most essential building blocks of financial security. It acts as a safety net, providing a cushion to handle unexpected expenses or financial disruptions. For single women planning their retirement, establishing an emergency fund is crucial. It not only protects against unforeseen events but also ensures that other financial goals, like retirement savings, stay on track.

The purpose of an emergency fund is simple: to provide financial support during unexpected situations, such as medical emergencies, car repairs, or sudden job loss. Without one, people often rely on high-interest loans or credit cards, which can lead to debt and disrupt long-term financial plans. By having an emergency fund in place, you can handle these surprises without derailing your budget or financial goals.

To start building an emergency fund, the first step is determining how much you need to save. Financial experts typically recommend setting aside three to six months' worth of essential living expenses. This amount varies depending on your lifestyle, monthly income, and level of financial responsibility. For instance, if your monthly expenses for housing, food, transportation, and utilities are $2,000, your emergency fund should ideally range between $6,000 and $12,000. If you work in an unstable industry or are self-employed, saving closer to six months' worth or even more may be wise.

Once you have a target amount, the next step is creating a plan to achieve it. Start by analyzing your current income and expenses. Identify areas where you can cut back to free up money for savings. For example, consider reducing discretionary spending, such as dining out, subscription services, or entertainment. Even small adjustments, like brewing your coffee at home instead of buying it daily, can add up over time.

Consistency is key when building an emergency fund. Set up a separate savings account specifically for this purpose to keep the money safe and accessible. Ideally, choose a high-yield savings account that earns interest, helping your funds grow faster. Automating your savings is another effective strategy. By scheduling automatic transfers from your checking account to your emergency fund, you remove the temptation to spend that money elsewhere. Even saving a modest amount, like $50 or $100 per month, can make a significant difference over time.

It's important to recognize that building an emergency fund takes time. Patience and persistence are essential, especially if you're starting from scratch. Break your goal into smaller, manageable milestones. For example, focus first on saving one month's worth of expenses, then work toward three months, and eventually aim for six months or more. Celebrating these milestones can help you stay motivated throughout the process.

An emergency fund should be easily accessible in case of need, but not so accessible that you're tempted to dip into it for non-emergencies. Resist the urge to use this money for vacations, shopping, or other discretionary expenses. To help maintain discipline, remind yourself of the fund's purpose: to protect you during genuine financial emergencies.

It's also crucial to distinguish between true emergencies and ordinary expenses. For instance, replacing worn-out tires on your car may feel urgent, but it's a predictable expense that should be budgeted for separately. Genuine emergencies are typically unexpected and urgent, such as sudden medical bills or job loss. Maintaining this distinction ensures your emergency fund remains intact when you need it most.

Once your emergency fund is fully funded, continue monitoring and updating it as needed. Over time, your living expenses may change due to factors like inflation, changes in housing costs, or lifestyle adjustments. Reassess your target amount periodically to ensure it remains sufficient. If your monthly expenses increase, add to your emergency fund to maintain adequate coverage.

For single women, having a robust emergency fund offers peace of mind and financial independence. It's particularly important because, without a partner's income, you're solely responsible for managing unexpected costs. An emergency fund empowers you to handle financial surprises confidently, reducing stress and allowing you to focus on long-term goals like retirement planning.

In addition to financial stability, an emergency fund can provide emotional security. Knowing that you have a safety net can alleviate anxiety about the future. It fosters a sense of control over your finances and prepares you to navigate life's uncertainties with resilience and confidence.

If you're struggling to find extra money to save, consider creative ways to boost your income temporarily. For example, you could take on a part-time job, sell unused items, or monetize a hobby. Direct any additional earnings toward your emergency fund until you reach your goal.

Remember that building an emergency fund is an ongoing process. Life's circumstances can change, and you may need to tap into your fund at some point. If you use part of your emergency fund, prioritize replenishing it as soon as possible. Treat it as a top financial priority, alongside paying bills and saving for retirement.

Establishing an emergency fund is a vital step toward achieving financial security. It protects you from unexpected expenses, prevents debt accumulation, and keeps your financial goals on track. By setting a savings target, creating a plan, and staying disciplined, you can build a strong safety net that provides both financial and emotional stability. For single women, this fund is not just a practical tool—it's a powerful symbol of independence and preparedness.

Developing a Budget that Prioritizes Savings

Creating a budget that prioritizes savings is a critical step toward achieving financial stability and securing a comfortable retirement. A well-structured budget helps you allocate resources effectively, minimize wasteful spending, and ensure that saving for the future remains a top priority. For single women planning for retirement, this process empowers you to build wealth, maintain financial independence, and prepare for life's uncertainties.

Start by understanding your income and expenses. Gather all financial information, including your monthly earnings, any irregular income, and fixed and variable expenses. Fixed expenses are those that stay constant each month, such as rent, utilities, or insurance premiums. Variable expenses, like groceries, transportation, and entertainment, fluctuate based on your habits and needs. By categorizing these costs, you gain a clear picture of where your money is going.

Once you have a clear snapshot of your finances, the next step is identifying areas where you can reduce spending. Review your variable expenses to spot opportunities for savings. For example, consider cutting back on dining out, limiting subscriptions, or finding cost-effective alternatives for entertainment. Even small adjustments, such as cooking at home more often or using public transportation, can free up significant amounts over time.

With savings opportunities identified, it's time to prioritize your goals. Retirement savings should take precedence in your budget. Financial experts often recommend following the "pay yourself first" principle. This means setting aside a portion of your income for savings before allocating money to other expenses. Treat your retirement contributions like an essential bill that must be paid every month.

Deciding how much to save depends on your retirement goals and timeline. A common recommendation is to save at least 15–20% of your income for retirement. However, if you're starting late, you may need to save a higher percentage to catch up. Use online retirement calculators to estimate how much you need based on your desired lifestyle, projected living costs, and expected years in retirement.

Automating your savings is an effective way to stay consistent. Set up automatic transfers from your checking account to a retirement account or savings account. This ensures that a portion of your income is saved without requiring manual effort, reducing the temptation to spend it elsewhere. By making savings automatic, you create a habit of consistently working toward your financial goals.

In addition to retirement savings, prioritize building an emergency fund within your budget. This fund provides a financial safety net for unexpected expenses, such as medical bills or car repairs, ensuring that you don't have to dip into retirement savings during emergencies. Allocate a portion of your budget to gradually grow this fund until it covers three to six months of living expenses.

When designing your budget, incorporate the 50/30/20 rule as a guideline. This rule suggests allocating 50% of your income to necessities (like housing and utilities), 30% to discretionary spending (like entertainment and dining out), and 20% to savings and debt repayment. For single women focused on retirement, consider adjusting these percentages to prioritize savings further; such as allocating 25% or more to savings if possible.

Tracking your spending is essential to ensure your budget is working effectively. Use budgeting tools, apps, or spreadsheets to monitor your expenses regularly. By reviewing your spending habits, you can identify areas where you're overspending and make adjustments as needed. This practice also helps you stay accountable to your financial goals.

To make your budget sustainable, allow for flexibility. Life is unpredictable, and your financial needs may change over time. If unexpected expenses arise or your income fluctuates, adapt your budget accordingly while maintaining a focus on savings. Flexibility ensures that your budget remains realistic and manageable in the long term.

Another important aspect of budgeting is finding ways to increase your income. If your current income makes it difficult to save enough, explore opportunities to earn more. This could include seeking a higher-paying job, taking on freelance work, or developing a side hustle based on your skills and interests. Direct any additional income toward your retirement savings to accelerate your progress.

As you implement your budget, set short-term and long-term milestones to track your progress. For example, aim to save a specific amount within six months or reach a percentage of your overall retirement goal within a year. Celebrating these milestones can keep you motivated and reinforce positive financial habits.

Avoid common budgeting mistakes, such as underestimating expenses or neglecting irregular costs like annual insurance premiums or holiday spending. Account for these expenses in your budget to prevent financial surprises. Additionally, resist the urge to adjust your budget every time your income increases, this is an opportunity to boost your savings rather than expand your spending.

Stay committed to your budgeting process. Building a budget that prioritizes savings requires discipline and consistency, but the rewards are worth the effort. Over time, you'll develop strong financial habits that not only support your retirement goals but also enhance your overall financial well-being.

Developing a budget that prioritizes savings involves understanding your finances, identifying opportunities to cut expenses, and automating your savings. By consistently tracking your spending, setting realistic goals, and maintaining flexibility, you can create a sustainable budget that keeps you on the path to a secure and comfortable retirement. This proactive approach empowers single women to take control of their financial futures with confidence and independence.

CHAPTER 3

Maximizing Income and Investments

Exploring Career Growth and Income Opportunities

Increasing your income is one of the most effective ways to enhance your financial security and prepare for retirement. For single women, exploring career growth and additional income opportunities can provide the financial freedom to save more, invest wisely, and meet long-term goals. Achieving this requires strategic planning, continuous learning, and exploring diverse avenues for earning.

Career advancement is a cornerstone for growing your income. Begin by evaluating your current job role and the opportunities available within your field. Understand what skills, certifications, or experience are required to move to the next level. Upskilling is often key to unlocking better roles and higher pay. Consider taking courses, attending workshops, or obtaining professional certifications that are relevant to your industry. Online platforms, universities, and industry associations offer numerous programs to help you stay competitive and broaden your skill set.

Networking plays a vital role in career growth. Build meaningful connections with colleagues, mentors, and industry professionals. Attend conferences, seminars, and industry events to meet influential people who can guide you or inform you about new opportunities. LinkedIn and similar professional networks are excellent tools for connecting with others and showcasing your skills and accomplishments.

Requesting a raise or negotiating your salary can also significantly increase your income. Before doing so, research salary ranges for your position in your area and gather data on your contributions to the company. Clearly articulate how your work has positively impacted the organization, whether through revenue generation, cost savings, or improving efficiency. Approach the conversation professionally and with confidence. Regularly assessing your market value and advocating for fair compensation ensures you're being paid appropriately for your expertise.

If you've reached a plateau in your current job, consider exploring new roles or even transitioning to a different career path. Changing industries or pursuing roles in high-demand fields can provide greater financial rewards. Seek guidance from career coaches or mentors if you're unsure of the best steps to take. Keep in mind that calculated risks, such as relocating or shifting to a new job, can sometimes lead to significant growth.

Side hustles are an increasingly popular way to generate additional income. These are flexible, often part-time opportunities that you can pursue alongside your primary job. Side hustles range from freelancing, tutoring, and consulting to running an online store or providing services like photography or event planning. Choose a side hustle that aligns with your skills and interests, as this increases your chances of success and enjoyment.

Freelancing is a particularly attractive option for those with specialized skills. Platforms like Upwork, Fiverr, and Freelancer allow you to offer services such as graphic design, writing, programming, or virtual assistance to clients worldwide. Freelancing provides flexibility, enabling you to manage your schedule while earning additional income.

Another potential avenue is turning hobbies into profitable ventures. If you have a passion for baking, crafting, or gardening, consider monetizing it. For instance, you could sell handmade items online, offer baking classes, or grow and sell plants.

Leveraging your hobbies not only creates an income stream but also brings personal satisfaction.

For those with an entrepreneurial mindset, starting a small business can be a lucrative option. Assess market needs in your community or online and identify gaps you can fill. For example, a tutoring service for students, pet sitting, or an eco-friendly product line can cater to specific demands. Although starting a business requires effort and planning, it can become a significant source of income over time.

Real estate is another way to maximize earnings. While it requires a substantial upfront investment, owning rental properties or engaging in short-term rentals can provide consistent passive income. If investing directly in property isn't feasible, consider real estate investment trusts that allow you to earn from real estate markets without owning physical property.

Additionally, using your current financial resources wisely can increase your overall income. Investing in stocks, bonds, mutual funds, or retirement accounts can generate returns that grow your wealth over time. Diversify your portfolio to balance risk and reward and consult a financial advisor if you're unsure about investment strategies.

Gig economy platforms such as ride-sharing, food delivery, and task-based apps offer flexible ways to earn extra cash. These roles typically don't require specialized skills and can be adjusted to fit your schedule. While these may not provide long-term career growth, they can supplement your income effectively.

Balancing your primary job, side hustle, or business with your personal life is essential to avoid burnout. Use tools like planners, productivity apps, and calendars to manage your time efficiently. Prioritize tasks and set realistic goals to ensure you're maintaining a healthy work-life balance.

It's also important to save and reinvest any additional income wisely. Allocate a portion of your earnings to retirement accounts, emergency funds, or investments. Avoid lifestyle inflation when income increases, focus on building financial security rather than increasing discretionary spending.

Stay informed about economic trends and opportunities in your field or industry. Keeping up with changes can help you spot new ways to grow your income. Continuously evaluate your progress and adapt your strategies to align with your goals.

Maximizing your income involves leveraging career growth opportunities, exploring side hustles, freelancing, and considering entrepreneurial ventures. By being proactive, building your skills, and effectively managing your time and resources, you can enhance your financial stability and achieve a secure retirement. These strategies empower single women to take control of their financial futures with confidence and independence.

Retirement Savings Vehicles: 401(k), IRA, and Beyond

Saving for retirement requires understanding the tools available to grow your wealth and secure your financial future. Retirement savings vehicles like 401(k)s, IRAs, and others are specifically designed to help individuals save and invest with tax advantages. By exploring these options, single women can identify the best strategies to maximize their savings and meet their retirement goals.

A 401(k) is one of the most common employer-sponsored retirement plans. Employers often offer 401(k)s as a benefit, allowing employees to contribute a portion of their income to the plan before taxes are deducted. This means your taxable income is reduced, which can lower your tax burden. Many employers also offer a matching contribution, effectively giving you free money for retirement. For example, if your employer matches up to 5% of your salary, contributing at least that amount ensures you maximize this benefit.

Investments within a 401(k) grow tax-deferred, meaning you don't pay taxes on the earnings until you withdraw funds during retirement. However, withdrawals before age 59½ typically incur penalties and taxes. If you change jobs, you can roll over your 401(k) into an IRA or another 401(k) plan to avoid penalties and maintain tax advantages.

An IRA, or Individual Retirement Account, is another powerful retirement savings option. Unlike a 401(k), an IRA isn't tied to an employer, making it a flexible choice for anyone, including freelancers and self-employed individuals. There are two main types of IRAs: Traditional and Roth.

With a Traditional IRA, your contributions may be tax-deductible, and like a 401(k), your investments grow tax-deferred. You'll pay taxes when you withdraw funds in retirement. This type of IRA is beneficial if you expect your income, and tax rate to be lower during retirement than it is now.

A Roth IRA, on the other hand, is funded with after-tax dollars. This means you don't get an immediate tax deduction, but your withdrawals in retirement, including earnings, are tax-free. Roth IRAs are especially advantageous if you expect your income to increase over time or if you prefer tax-free income in retirement. Unlike Traditional IRAs, Roth IRAs don't have required minimum distributions, allowing your money to grow longer.

Both Traditional and Roth IRAs have annual contribution limits, which the IRS adjusts periodically. For example, if the current limit is $6,500 for individuals under 50, you can only contribute that amount in a year. However, those aged 50 and older can make an additional "catch-up" contribution, allowing them to save more.

For those who are self-employed or own small businesses, a SEP IRA (Simplified Employee Pension) or a Solo 401(k) can provide higher contribution limits than a standard IRA. A SEP IRA is easy to set up and allows you to contribute up to 25% of your income, making it ideal for self-employed individuals. A Solo 401(k) offers similar benefits but also includes a Roth option, giving you more flexibility with your savings.

Another option to consider is an Health Savings Account, which isn't traditionally a retirement vehicle but can serve as one. Health Savings Account are available to individuals with high-deductible health insurance plans. Contributions to an Health Savings Account are tax-deductible, the money grows tax-free, and withdrawals for qualified medical expenses are tax-free. After age 65, you can use Health Savings Account funds for non-medical expenses without penalties, although they'll be taxed like a

Traditional IRA withdrawal. This makes an Health Savings Account a dual-purpose tool for healthcare and retirement savings.

Brokerage accounts, though not specifically retirement-focused, can also be used to build retirement savings. These accounts don't have the tax advantages of 401(k)s or IRAs, but they offer unlimited contributions and complete flexibility. You can invest in stocks, bonds, mutual funds, and Exchange-Traded Funds, withdrawing funds at any time without penalties. For individuals who want to save beyond the limits of traditional retirement accounts or require greater liquidity, a brokerage account can complement their retirement strategy.

Pension plans, though less common today, are another savings vehicle offered by some employers. These are defined benefit plans where the employer promises a specific monthly payment upon retirement, based on factors like your salary and years of service. If you have access to a pension, it's important to understand the terms and how it fits into your overall retirement plan.

Annuities are insurance products that can provide guaranteed income during retirement. There are several types of annuities, including fixed, variable, and indexed, each with unique benefits and risks. Annuities are purchased with a lump sum or through periodic payments and can offer a steady income stream, making them an attractive option for those seeking financial stability in retirement. However, they often come with high fees and less flexibility, so careful evaluation is essential.

When choosing the right retirement savings vehicle, consider your financial situation, goals, and timeline. If your employer offers a 401(k) with matching contributions, prioritize that first to take advantage of the free money. Then, if eligible, contribute to a Roth or Traditional IRA. If you're self-employed, explore SEP IRAs or Solo 401(k)s. For additional savings, consider Health Savings

Account, brokerage accounts, or annuities based on your needs.

Diversification is key to building a strong retirement plan. Don't rely solely on one account type or investment. Spreading your savings across multiple vehicles can reduce risk and provide flexibility in accessing funds. Monitor your accounts regularly, adjust contributions as your income grows, and consult a financial advisor to ensure your strategy remains aligned with your goals.

Understanding and utilizing these retirement savings vehicles is critical for single women aiming to achieve financial independence. Each option offers unique advantages, and by combining them wisely, you can create a robust plan tailored to your lifestyle and future needs.

Smart Investment Strategies for Long-term Growth

Investing is a powerful way to grow your money over time, especially for single women planning for retirement. Smart investment strategies combine careful planning, understanding risk, and focusing on long-term growth. By making informed decisions, you can build a diversified portfolio that balances potential returns with financial stability, ensuring your future security.

The first step to effective investing is understanding your financial goals and timeline. For retirement planning, long-term growth should be the primary focus. This means selecting investments that have the potential to increase in value over many years. Start by identifying when you plan to retire and how much money you'll need. These factors will help you decide the level of risk you can tolerate and the types of investments that align with your needs.

Diversification is one of the most critical principles of investing. This involves spreading your money across different asset classes, such as stocks, bonds, real estate, and mutual funds. By diversifying, you reduce the risk of losing everything if one type of investment performs poorly. For example, if the stock market declines, bonds or other assets in your portfolio may help balance the loss. A well-diversified portfolio provides stability and growth potential over the long term.

Stocks are a key component of any long-term investment strategy. They represent ownership in a company and can generate returns through price appreciation and dividends. While stocks are generally riskier than other investments, they offer the highest potential for growth over time. For single women planning for retirement, investing in a mix of large, stable companies (blue-chip stocks) and smaller, high-growth firms can provide a balanced approach. Consider using low-cost index funds or exchange-traded funds to gain exposure to a wide range of stocks without needing to pick individual companies.

Bonds are another essential part of a retirement portfolio. These are loans you make to governments or corporations in exchange for regular interest payments and the return of your principal when the bond matures. Bonds are typically less volatile than stocks, making them a good choice for managing risk. As you get closer to retirement, increasing your bond allocation can help protect your investments from market fluctuations.

Mutual funds and Exchange-Traded Funds are excellent tools for building a diversified portfolio. These funds pool money from many investors to buy a broad range of assets, such as stocks, bonds, or other securities. They are managed by professionals, which makes them a convenient option for those with limited investing experience. Exchange-Traded Funds, in particular, are a cost-effective way to invest, as they often have lower fees than mutual funds and can be traded like stocks.

Real estate investments can also play a role in long-term growth. Purchasing property for rental income or investing in real estate investment trusts provides opportunities for steady returns. Real estate tends to appreciate over time and can serve as a hedge against inflation. However, it requires careful research and management, so consider your expertise and time availability before committing.

For single women, managing investment risk is essential. Risk tolerance varies from person to person, depending on financial goals, age, and personal comfort. Younger investors typically have a higher tolerance for risk because they have more time to recover from market downturns. Older investors nearing retirement should focus on preserving capital by shifting toward lower-risk investments like bonds or cash equivalents.

Dollar-cost averaging is a smart strategy to reduce the impact of market volatility. This approach involves investing a fixed amount of money regularly, regardless of market conditions. By doing so, you buy more shares when prices are low and fewer shares when prices are high, which helps smooth out the cost over time and reduces the temptation to time the market.

Compounding is another powerful tool for long-term growth. When you reinvest your earnings, whether they come from dividends, interest, or capital gains, your money starts earning returns on its returns. Over time, this snowball effect significantly increases the value of your investments. Starting early and staying consistent are key to maximizing the benefits of compounding.

Avoiding common investment mistakes is crucial for success. Emotional decision-making, such as panic selling during a market downturn, can lead to significant losses. It's important to stick to your long-term plan and not be swayed by short-term fluctuations. High fees can also erode your returns, so look for low-cost investment options and monitor your accounts regularly.

Consider working with a financial advisor to develop a personalized investment strategy. An advisor can help you understand your risk tolerance, select appropriate investments, and adjust your portfolio as needed. For single women, finding an advisor who understands your unique financial goals and challenges can provide valuable guidance.

Stay informed and continually educate yourself about investing. Understanding the basics of how markets work and the options available to you empowers you to make better decisions. Read books, attend seminars, or take online courses to deepen your knowledge. The more you learn, the more confident you'll feel in managing your investments.

Smart investment strategies for long-term growth require careful planning, diversification, and consistent action. By focusing on a mix of stocks, bonds, real estate, and other assets, managing risk, and leveraging tools like compounding and dollar-cost averaging, you can build a strong financial foundation for your retirement. With patience and persistence, your investments will work for you, ensuring a secure and comfortable future.

CHAPTER 4

Planning for Health and Wellness

Budgeting for Healthcare Costs in Retirement

Planning for healthcare costs in retirement is an essential step in creating a secure financial future. Healthcare is often one of the largest expenses retirees face, and for single women, who may not have a partner's income or employer-provided coverage to rely on, careful preparation is vital. Understanding potential costs and setting aside sufficient funds can help ensure that you're not caught off guard by medical expenses later in life.

Start by assessing your current health and anticipating future needs. While it's impossible to predict every medical event, you can estimate costs based on your family history, lifestyle, and any existing health conditions. For example, if chronic conditions like diabetes or heart disease run in your family, you may need to allocate more for ongoing treatments or medications. Maintaining a healthy lifestyle now can reduce potential healthcare costs later, but it's still wise to budget for unforeseen issues.

Medicare is a critical resource for retirees, but it doesn't cover all healthcare costs. Many retirees mistakenly assume that Medicare will handle most expenses, only to discover significant gaps. Original Medicare (Part A and Part B) generally covers hospital stays, doctor visits, and some preventive services but excludes dental, vision, hearing aids, and long-term care. To fill these gaps, you might need supplemental insurance, such as Medigap, or a Medicare Advantage Plan. Research these options thoroughly to understand their costs and benefits.

Another important consideration is prescription drug coverage. Medicare Part D helps cover the cost of medications, but the out-of-pocket expenses can still add up, especially if you require multiple prescriptions or specialized drugs. Reviewing the Medicare Part D formulary annually to ensure your medications are covered can save you money. Additionally, ask your doctor about generic alternatives or assistance programs to lower costs.

Long-term care is a significant and often overlooked expense. This type of care includes services like nursing homes, assisted living facilities, and in-home care, which are not covered by Medicare. Long-term care insurance is one option to help cover these costs, but premiums can be expensive, especially if purchased later in life. Begin exploring this coverage early, ideally in your 50s or early 60s, when premiums are more affordable.

Creating a dedicated healthcare savings fund can help you manage these expenses. A Health Savings Account is a powerful tool for those still working and enrolled in a high-deductible health plan. Health Savings Account offer triple tax advantages: contributions are tax-deductible, growth is tax-free, and withdrawals for qualified medical expenses are not taxed. Even in retirement, Health Savings Account funds can be used for Medicare premiums and other healthcare costs.

Inflation is another factor to consider when budgeting for healthcare in retirement. Medical expenses tend to rise faster than general inflation, which means the amount you save today may not be sufficient in the future. Using conservative estimates when planning can help you stay prepared for these increases. For instance, if healthcare costs currently represent 15% of your retirement budget, plan for that percentage to grow over time.

Preventive care and wellness practices are also essential parts of managing healthcare costs. Regular check-ups, vaccinations, and screenings can help detect issues early and prevent more expensive treatments down the line. Staying active, eating a balanced diet, and managing stress can improve your overall health and reduce the likelihood of costly medical conditions.

Understanding and managing end-of-life care expenses is another crucial aspect of retirement planning. Hospice care, palliative care, and other related services can be emotionally and financially draining. Discussing these matters with family members and creating advance directives or living wills can help ensure your wishes are respected and reduce the financial burden on loved ones.

It's also essential to review your healthcare budget periodically. Life circumstances, medical needs, and policy changes can all affect your expenses. Schedule an annual review of your budget to ensure it aligns with your current and anticipated healthcare needs. Adjust your savings and spending as necessary to stay on track.

Seek professional advice when planning for healthcare costs in retirement. A financial planner or insurance specialist with expertise in retirement can provide personalized guidance based on your situation. They can help you estimate expenses, compare insurance plans, and develop a comprehensive strategy to address your healthcare needs.

Planning for healthcare costs in retirement requires foresight, discipline, and adaptability. By estimating potential expenses, exploring insurance options, and maintaining a healthy lifestyle, you can prepare for this significant aspect of retirement. With a clear strategy and sufficient savings, you'll be well-equipped to manage healthcare costs and enjoy peace of mind in your golden years.

Choosing the Right Insurance Plans

Choosing the right insurance plans is a crucial part of retirement planning, especially for single women. Insurance acts as a financial safety net, protecting you from unexpected expenses that could jeopardize your savings. Selecting appropriate plans involves understanding your needs, comparing options, and planning for long-term security. Key types of insurance to consider include health insurance, long-term care insurance, and supplemental plans tailored to your unique situation.

Health insurance is the cornerstone of financial protection in retirement. For most retirees in the United States, Medicare becomes the primary health coverage starting at age 65. However, Medicare is not a one-size-fits-all program. Original Medicare includes Part A (hospital coverage) and Part B (medical services), but it leaves significant gaps, such as no coverage for dental, vision, hearing aids, or most prescription drugs. To address these gaps, you might need to consider Medicare Advantage

Plans or Medigap policies. Medicare Advantage Plans, also known as Part C, often bundle additional services like dental and vision coverage, but they may have network restrictions. Medigap policies are supplemental plans that help pay for out-of-pocket costs like deductibles and co-pays, offering more flexibility in choosing providers.

Prescription drug coverage is another essential component of health insurance. Medicare Part D provides this coverage, but each plan's formulary (list of covered medications) differs. To choose the best Part D plan, review the medications you currently take and compare plan costs, including premiums, co-pays, and coverage limits. Annual reviews of your Part D plan can help you adapt to changes in your medication needs or plan formularies.

Long-term care insurance is another critical consideration for single women, as it helps cover the costs of services like nursing homes, assisted living facilities, or in-home care. Women tend to live longer than men, increasing the likelihood of needing long-term care. Since Medicare does not cover most long-term care expenses, having a dedicated plan is essential. Long-term care insurance policies vary widely in coverage and cost, so it's important to assess your potential needs early. Consider factors like daily benefit amounts, the duration of coverage, and whether the policy includes inflation protection to keep up with rising healthcare costs.

Disability insurance is often overlooked but can be invaluable if you're still working and something affects your ability to earn income. While Social Security Disability Insurance is available, the benefits might not be sufficient to maintain your lifestyle. Private disability insurance offers more comprehensive protection and can bridge the gap between income loss and retirement savings.

Life insurance is another type of policy to evaluate, even if you don't have dependents. Some single women use life insurance as part of their estate planning, ensuring that their assets can cover outstanding debts, charitable donations, or caregiving for elderly parents. Whole life insurance can also serve as a financial tool, building cash value over time that you can borrow against in emergencies.

When selecting insurance plans, cost is an important factor. Premiums, deductibles, co-pays, and coverage limits all contribute to the overall expense of a policy. Calculate how much you can afford to spend without compromising other retirement goals. Comparing multiple plans from reputable providers can help you find the best balance between cost and coverage. Use online tools, consult insurance brokers, or seek advice from a financial planner to navigate these choices.

Another consideration is the policy's flexibility. Some plans allow adjustments as your needs change. For example, long-term care policies with hybrid options combine traditional benefits with life insurance or annuities, providing more value for your investment. Flexible policies can be particularly beneficial if you're uncertain about your future needs.

It's also crucial to understand the terms and exclusions of any policy you're considering. Read the fine print carefully to avoid surprises. For example, some health insurance plans may exclude pre-existing conditions or impose waiting periods for certain benefits. Similarly, long-term care policies may require proof of medical need before coverage begins.

Timing your purchase of insurance is another strategic decision. Health and long-term care insurance premiums are generally lower when purchased at a younger age and while you're in good health. Delaying could result in higher costs or even denial of coverage due to age or health conditions.

As you assess your insurance needs, think about your support network. Single women often rely on friends, family, or professional caregivers in retirement. If you anticipate needing significant support, ensure your insurance covers the types of care you're likely to require. For instance, policies that include in-home care benefits might align better with your preferences for aging in place.

Don't hesitate to seek professional guidance when navigating the complexities of insurance. An experienced financial advisor or insurance specialist can help you tailor a plan to your needs and budget. They can also keep you informed about changes in insurance regulations or new products that might benefit you.

Choosing the right insurance plans is not just about preparing for the worst but also about ensuring peace of mind. By carefully evaluating your needs, exploring your options, and planning strategically, you can create a safety net that protects your retirement savings and supports a secure, comfortable future.

Strategies for Maintaining Physical and Mental Health

Maintaining physical and mental health during retirement is essential for leading a fulfilling and independent life. Retirement brings more freedom and time, but it also requires a proactive approach to well-being. Balancing physical activity, a nutritious diet, and mental health strategies can ensure you remain active, energized, and resilient.

Physical health forms the foundation of a happy retirement. Regular exercise is a key component and doesn't have to involve strenuous activities. Simple routines like daily walking, yoga, or swimming can improve cardiovascular health, strengthen muscles, and enhance flexibility. Strength training, even with light weights, can help maintain bone density and reduce the risk of osteoporosis. For single women, group classes or community fitness programs can be an excellent way to stay active while building social connections.

Nutrition is equally important in maintaining physical health. A balanced diet rich in fruits, vegetables, whole grains, lean proteins, and healthy fats can provide the energy and nutrients your body needs. Portion control and mindful eating can help prevent overeating and maintain a healthy weight. Staying hydrated is also essential, as dehydration can lead to fatigue, confusion, and other health issues. Limiting processed foods, added sugars, and excessive salt intake can reduce the risk of chronic conditions such as diabetes and high blood pressure.

Regular health check-ups and screenings are vital for early detection of potential issues. Preventative care, including vaccines, mammograms, bone density tests, and cholesterol monitoring, can help identify and address problems before they become serious. Maintaining a good relationship with your healthcare provider ensures that your medical history and preferences are well-understood, leading to more personalized care.

Mental health is just as crucial as physical health in retirement. Keeping your mind active and engaged can prevent cognitive decline and enhance your quality of life. Activities like reading, puzzles, and learning new skills stimulate the brain. Consider taking up a hobby or exploring creative outlets such as painting, writing, or gardening, which can be both relaxing and rewarding.

Social connections play a significant role in mental well-being. Engaging with friends, family, or community groups helps combat loneliness and creates a sense of belonging. Volunteering is another excellent way to stay connected while giving back to the community. Many organizations actively seek the wisdom and experience that retirees bring.

Stress management is an essential part of mental health. Retirement can bring unexpected challenges, such as financial concerns or adjusting to a new routine. Practicing mindfulness, meditation, or deep breathing exercises can help you stay calm and focused. Setting aside time each day for relaxation and self-care ensures that you prioritize your well-being amidst daily responsibilities.

Getting enough sleep is critical for overall health. Aim for 7-9 hours of quality sleep each night. Establishing a consistent bedtime routine, limiting screen time before bed, and creating a comfortable sleep environment can help improve sleep quality. Sleep not only rejuvenates your body but also enhances memory, mood, and problem-solving abilities.

Developing a positive mindset is a cornerstone of mental health during retirement. Embracing gratitude and focusing on what you can control fosters resilience. Celebrate your achievements, no matter how small, and give yourself grace during challenging times. Journaling can be a helpful tool for processing emotions and reflecting on your journey.

Maintaining a sense of purpose can greatly enhance mental health. Retirement is an opportunity to align your life with your values and passions. Whether it's mentoring younger generations, pursuing a lifelong dream, or dedicating time to causes you care about, having a clear sense of purpose adds meaning to your days.

Physical and mental health are deeply interconnected, and adopting a holistic approach benefits both. Regular exercise not only strengthens the body but also releases endorphins that improve mood and reduce stress. Eating nutritious meals supports brain function, while socializing boosts emotional well-being. Combining these strategies creates a positive cycle of health and happiness.

Acknowledge the importance of adaptability. Health needs evolve over time, and being open to adjusting your strategies ensures that you stay on track. Whether it's incorporating new exercises, exploring different relaxation techniques, or seeking support from professionals, flexibility allows you to navigate the ups and downs of retirement with confidence.

Retirement is a chapter full of opportunities to prioritize yourself. By taking active steps to maintain physical and mental health, you can enjoy this stage of life to the fullest. A strong body and mind empower you to pursue your interests, connect with loved ones, and savor the rewards of your hard work and planning.

CHAPTER 5

Housing and Living Arrangements

Evaluating Your Housing Options: Downsizing or Relocating

Choosing the right housing option during retirement is a significant decision that impacts financial stability, physical well-being, and emotional health. Whether you decide to downsize, relocate, or remain in your current home, each choice comes with distinct advantages and challenges. Carefully evaluating these options ensures your living arrangements align with your retirement goals and lifestyle preferences.

Downsizing is a popular choice for retirees seeking to simplify their lives and reduce expenses. Moving to a smaller home often leads to lower utility bills, property taxes, and maintenance costs. Additionally, a smaller living space can be easier to clean and manage, which is especially beneficial as mobility or energy levels change with age. Selling a larger home and purchasing a smaller one can also free up equity, providing additional funds to bolster your retirement savings or cover unexpected expenses.

Beyond financial benefits, downsizing can promote a sense of liberation. Letting go of excess belongings and focusing on what truly matters fosters a minimalist lifestyle that prioritizes experiences over possessions. However, the downsizing process can be emotionally taxing, particularly when parting with items tied to cherished memories. It's essential to plan ahead, involve family members for support, and approach the process gradually to ease the transition.

Relocating offers retirees the opportunity to embrace a new environment that aligns with their desired lifestyle. Some retirees move to be closer to family and friends, creating opportunities for stronger relationships and a reliable support network. Others may relocate to regions with a lower cost of living, allowing their retirement savings to stretch further. Warmer climates and retirement-friendly communities are also attractive options, offering amenities such as recreational activities, healthcare facilities, and social clubs designed for seniors.

While relocation has its appeal, it's not without challenges. Adapting to a new community can take time, and leaving familiar surroundings might feel isolating initially. Researching potential destinations thoroughly is crucial. Consider factors such as healthcare access, climate, safety, and local tax policies. Visiting the area multiple times before making a permanent move can help ensure it feels like the right fit. Additionally, involve trusted advisors to evaluate the financial implications of the relocation, including the cost of moving and property purchases.

For some retirees, staying in their current home is the most appealing option. Remaining in a familiar space can provide comfort and stability, allowing retirees to maintain existing routines and social connections. Those with homes in good condition and accessible layouts may find it more practical to age in place. Home modifications, such as installing grab bars, widening doorways, or adding stairlifts, can improve safety and make the home more accommodating as physical needs evolve.

However, staying put may require ongoing financial planning to address maintenance costs, property taxes, and utilities. Retirees should also consider proximity to essential services like grocery stores, healthcare providers, and public transportation. If these services are lacking, additional support from family, friends, or hired caregivers might be necessary.

Weighing the pros and cons of each housing option involves more than just financial calculations. Emotional and social factors play a vital role in determining the best fit. Downsizing may appeal to those seeking simplicity and reduced expenses, but it requires a willingness to adapt to a smaller space. Relocation might bring new adventures and opportunities, yet it demands careful planning and the ability to adjust to a different environment. Staying put offers familiarity and stability but may require investments in home modifications and access to local resources.

Creating a detailed plan can help simplify the decision-making process. Begin by listing your priorities, such as financial security, accessibility, proximity to loved ones, and access to amenities. Consult with financial advisors, real estate professionals, and healthcare providers to gain a comprehensive understanding of how each option aligns with your needs. Engaging in open discussions with family members can also provide valuable insights and support.

Housing decisions during retirement should also consider the long-term. Your needs may change as you age, so it's wise to explore options that offer flexibility. For instance, moving to a retirement community that provides independent living, assisted living, and skilled nursing care can ensure you're prepared for any future health challenges. These communities often foster social engagement and provide on-site services, offering a balanced blend of independence and support.

The right housing choice will depend on your unique circumstances and goals. Whether you decide to downsize, relocate, or remain in your current home, the key is to make an informed decision that prioritizes comfort, safety, and financial stability. Retirement is a time to embrace new opportunities, and choosing the right living arrangement sets the foundation for a secure and fulfilling future.

Creating a Safe and Comfortable Living Environment

Creating a safe and comfortable living environment during retirement is essential for ensuring well-being and peace of mind. As individuals age, their physical and emotional needs evolve, making it crucial to design a home that supports their lifestyle, prioritizes safety, and promotes ease of access. Whether you're adapting an existing home or planning to move into a new one, thoughtful adjustments can make your living space a haven of comfort and security.

Safety is the cornerstone of a retirement-friendly home. Eliminating potential hazards helps prevent accidents and creates a stress-free environment. Start by assessing areas that pose risks, such as slippery floors, uneven surfaces, or poorly lit spaces. Installing non-slip mats or flooring, particularly in the kitchen and bathroom, can significantly reduce the likelihood of falls. Ensuring that rugs are securely anchored to the floor and eliminating clutter in pathways also minimizes tripping hazards.

Handrails and grab bars are essential additions, especially in areas like staircases, bathrooms, and hallways. These provide stability and support, making it easier to move around the house safely. In bathrooms, consider installing walk-in tubs or showers with anti-slip surfaces. Adding a shower chair or adjustable handheld showerhead can enhance comfort and safety during daily routines. Lever-style faucets and doorknobs are also more accessible for individuals with arthritis or reduced grip strength.

Proper lighting plays a crucial role in maintaining a safe living environment. Bright, even lighting ensures visibility and helps prevent missteps. Motion-sensor lights are particularly helpful in hallways, entryways, and bathrooms, as they eliminate the need to fumble for switches in the dark. Place nightlights in frequently used areas like bedrooms, bathrooms, and kitchens to provide gentle illumination during nighttime.

Comfort is another vital aspect of a retirement-friendly home. Comfortable furniture that supports good posture and is easy to get in and out of can improve overall quality of life. Look for chairs and sofas with firm cushions, sturdy armrests, and the right seat height to reduce strain on joints. Adjustable beds or recliners can offer added relaxation and adaptability for various needs.

Temperature control also contributes to a cozy and enjoyable home environment. Installing a programmable thermostat allows you to maintain an optimal temperature without constant manual adjustments. Ensure that windows are well-sealed and insulated to prevent drafts and maintain consistent indoor temperatures, especially during extreme weather conditions.

Accessibility is key to creating a home that supports independence and ease of movement. Wide doorways and hallways accommodate mobility aids like wheelchairs and walkers. Ramps or stairlifts are valuable additions for multi-level homes, while a single-story layout eliminates the challenge of navigating stairs altogether. Ensure that frequently used items, such as kitchen tools or toiletries, are stored at accessible heights to avoid unnecessary reaching or bending.

Technology can enhance both safety and convenience in your living space. Smart home devices, such as voice-activated assistants, can control lighting, appliances, and security systems with ease. Emergency alert systems, which allow for quick communication with loved ones or medical services, provide an additional layer of security. Video doorbells and home security cameras offer peace of mind by monitoring your property and identifying visitors.

The layout of your home also affects its functionality and livability. Open floor plans with minimal barriers between rooms create a sense of spaciousness and allow for easy navigation. Creating dedicated spaces for relaxation, hobbies, and socializing helps foster a balanced lifestyle. For example, a reading nook with good lighting and a comfortable chair can serve as a retreat, while a well-organized craft or workspace encourages creativity.

Incorporating nature into your living environment can have positive effects on mental and emotional well-being. If possible, create an outdoor space, such as a garden or patio, where you can enjoy fresh air and sunlight. Indoor plants can also bring a touch of greenery indoors, improving air quality and creating a calming atmosphere.

Financial considerations are an important part of designing a safe and comfortable home. While some modifications may require an initial investment, they often save money in the long run by preventing injuries and reducing maintenance costs. Research grants, loans, or community programs that may assist with the cost of home improvements for retirees. Consulting with a professional, such as an occupational therapist or contractor, can help identify the most effective and affordable solutions.

Designing a home that accommodates future needs ensures long-term comfort and security. Even if you don't currently require mobility aids or other support, planning ahead can save time and money later. Universal design principles, which focus on creating spaces that are usable by everyone regardless of age or ability, offer a practical approach to future-proofing your home.

By prioritizing safety, comfort, and accessibility, you can create a living environment that supports a fulfilling and independent retirement. Thoughtful planning and attention to detail ensure that your home becomes a sanctuary where you can thrive during this exciting chapter of life.

Planning for Long-term Care and Assisted Living

Planning for long-term care and assisted living is a critical part of preparing for retirement, as these services address potential health challenges and support needs that may arise with aging. Understanding the different options available and their associated costs ensures that you are financially prepared while maintaining a high quality of life. Thoughtful planning provides peace of mind and preserves independence for as long as possible.

Long-term care refers to a range of services designed to assist individuals with daily activities such as bathing, dressing, eating, or mobility. These services can be provided in various settings, including your home, community centers, or specialized facilities like assisted living residences or nursing homes. The level of care needed depends on individual circumstances, such as health conditions, mobility, or cognitive abilities.

One of the first steps in planning for long-term care is assessing your potential needs. Consider your family health history, current medical conditions, and lifestyle factors. For instance, individuals with a family history of chronic illnesses, such as dementia or arthritis, may be more likely to require extended care. This evaluation helps identify the type and duration of care that might be necessary, enabling you to make informed decisions.

Costs are a significant factor in long-term care planning. The expenses vary widely depending on the type of care, location, and duration. For example, in-home care services, such as a caregiver or nurse, may be less expensive than a full-time stay in a nursing home. However, as the level of care increases, costs can escalate. It's essential to research and understand the average costs of services in your area to prepare adequately.

Long-term care insurance is a valuable tool for managing these expenses. This type of insurance covers a portion of the costs associated with extended care, reducing the financial burden on you and your family. When selecting a policy, pay attention to the coverage details, such as the type of services included, daily benefit limits, and waiting periods. Purchasing long-term care insurance early, when you are in good health, can result in lower premiums and broader coverage options.

For those who do not qualify for or cannot afford long-term care insurance, alternative funding options are available. Personal savings, government programs like Medicaid, and veteran benefits can help cover costs. Medicaid, for instance, provides assistance for low-income individuals but typically requires meeting specific eligibility criteria, including income and asset limits. Familiarize yourself with these options and understand how they align with your financial situation.

Assisted living is a popular choice for individuals who require some level of assistance but wish to maintain an independent lifestyle. These facilities provide housing, meals, social activities, and support with daily tasks, making them a middle ground between living at home and a nursing home. When considering assisted living, visit multiple facilities to evaluate their quality, amenities, and staff-to-resident ratios. Ask about licensing, safety measures, and healthcare services to ensure the environment aligns with your needs and preferences.

If aging in place remaining in your own home is your preferred option, modifications to your living environment may be necessary. Installing grab bars, wheelchair ramps, or stairlifts enhances accessibility and safety. Additionally, hiring in-home care services allows you to receive professional support without relocating. Keep in mind that while aging in place offers comfort and familiarity, it can become costly if advanced medical care is required.

Discussing long-term care plans with family members is crucial, even if you are single. Close relatives or trusted friends can play a significant role in decision-making and providing emotional or logistical support. Open communication ensures that everyone involved understands your wishes and is prepared to honor them. This step can also help identify potential caregivers or decision-makers if the need arises.

Legal and financial preparations are equally important. Create or update documents such as a will, power of attorney, and healthcare proxy to outline your preferences for medical care and financial decisions. These documents empower a trusted individual to act on your behalf if you are unable to make decisions independently. Consulting with an attorney who specializes in elder law can help ensure that your plans are comprehensive and legally sound.

Exploring community resources and programs can also enhance long-term care planning. Many communities offer services such as adult daycare centers, meal delivery programs, and transportation assistance for seniors. These resources can reduce reliance on costly professional care while maintaining a high quality of life. Research local organizations and services to identify those that may benefit you.

Flexibility is key to effective planning. As your circumstances change, your care needs may evolve, requiring adjustments to your original plan. Regularly review your financial situation, insurance policies, and health status to ensure your plan remains relevant. Being proactive about these updates minimizes stress and allows for a smoother transition if care needs increase.

Remember that long-term care planning is not just about preparing for potential challenges, it's about safeguarding your independence, dignity, and well-being in the later stages of life. By addressing this aspect of retirement planning early and comprehensively, you can enjoy peace of mind, knowing that you are prepared for whatever the future holds.

CHAPTER 6

Creating a Meaningful Lifestyle

Identifying Your Passions and Hobbies

Identifying your passions and hobbies is a vital step in creating a meaningful and fulfilling retirement. After years of work and responsibilities, retirement offers a unique opportunity to focus on personal interests and activities that bring joy and purpose to your life. Pursuing hobbies can enhance your mental, emotional, and even physical well-being while providing opportunities to connect with others and explore your creativity.

The first step in identifying your passions is self-reflection. Think about activities you've enjoyed in the past but may not have had time to pursue. These could include artistic endeavors like painting or writing, physical activities like gardening or hiking, or intellectual pursuits like reading and solving puzzles. Reflect on what makes you feel excited, energized, or at peace. Consider writing down these ideas to create a list of potential interests.

Exploring new activities is another excellent way to discover hobbies that resonate with you. Retirement is the perfect time to step out of your comfort zone and try something you've never done before. You might take a cooking class, learn a new language, or experiment with photography. Engaging in new experiences not only broadens your horizons but also keeps your mind active and stimulated, which is crucial for maintaining cognitive health as you age.

It's also important to evaluate how your hobbies align with your personal values and goals. For example, if you value community involvement, you might find fulfillment in volunteering or joining a local club. If environmental sustainability is important to you, consider hobbies like upcycling or participating in local conservation efforts. By aligning your activities with your values, you can create a deeper sense of purpose and satisfaction.

Cultivating hobbies doesn't always require significant financial investment. Many activities, such as writing, drawing, or exploring nature, are low-cost or even free. Libraries, community centers, and online platforms offer numerous resources for learning new skills or joining interest-based groups without spending a fortune. Look for affordable opportunities in your area that align with your interests and budget.

Hobbies that involve physical activity can also contribute to your overall health and well-being. Activities like yoga, dancing, or tai chi promote flexibility, strength, and balance while providing mental relaxation. Outdoor hobbies such as birdwatching, gardening, or cycling allow you to connect with nature and improve cardiovascular health. Incorporating physical movement into your hobbies helps maintain a healthy lifestyle and reduces the risk of age-related health issues.

Social hobbies are particularly beneficial for emotional health. Joining clubs, participating in group classes, or attending meet-ups can help you build friendships and combat loneliness, which is a common challenge during retirement. Shared interests create meaningful connections, making it easier to form bonds with like-minded individuals. Whether it's a book club, a knitting circle, or a hiking group, being part of a community enriches your social life.

If you have skills or knowledge in a specific area, consider turning them into hobbies that also benefit others. For instance, you could tutor students, mentor young professionals, or share your expertise through workshops or blogs. Teaching and mentoring not only allow you to share your passion but also give you a sense of accomplishment and legacy.

Journaling can be a useful tool in identifying and refining your passions. Writing about your interests, dreams, and daily activities can reveal patterns and preferences that you might not have noticed otherwise. It can also help you track your progress and celebrate milestones in your hobbies, boosting your motivation and confidence.

Incorporating creativity into your hobbies adds another layer of fulfillment. Creative activities such as painting, crafting, or playing a musical instrument stimulate the brain and allow you to express yourself in unique ways. Creativity fosters a sense of achievement and provides a healthy outlet for emotions, reducing stress and enhancing mental clarity.

For those who enjoy learning, retirement is an excellent time to dive deeper into areas of interest. Online courses, local workshops, and adult education programs offer opportunities to expand your knowledge and skills. You might explore subjects like history, science, or technology, or even pursue a certification in an area you're passionate about. Lifelong learning keeps your mind sharp and ensures that you continue to grow intellectually.

Remember that your passions and hobbies can evolve over time. What interests you today might not hold the same appeal in a few years, and that's perfectly fine. Stay open to exploring new activities and adapting your interests as your preferences change. Flexibility ensures that your retirement remains dynamic and engaging.

By dedicating time to discovering and cultivating your passions, you create a foundation for a meaningful and enjoyable retirement. Hobbies provide a sense of purpose, structure, and joy, making your retirement years not just a time of rest but a time of personal growth and fulfillment.

Building a Support Network and Social Connections

Building a support network and maintaining strong social connections is essential for a happy and fulfilling retirement. Social connections enrich your life by providing companionship, emotional support, and a sense of belonging. They can also play a significant role in improving mental and physical health. As you transition into retirement, focusing on nurturing relationships and creating a reliable support network is a key step in ensuring your well-being and happiness.

Social connections start with meaningful relationships. These can include family, friends, neighbors, and community members. It's important to evaluate your current relationships and identify those that bring positivity and encouragement into your life. Strengthening these relationships can involve regular communication, shared activities, and acts of kindness. Simple gestures like checking in, sharing meals, or attending events together can deepen bonds and make people feel valued.

Retirement offers the opportunity to expand your social circle. Joining clubs, interest groups, or volunteering organizations can introduce you to like-minded individuals who share your passions and hobbies. For example, if you enjoy gardening, a local horticulture club could connect you with others who share your enthusiasm. Volunteering at community centers, schools, or non-profits not only allows you to give back but also creates chances to meet people with shared values.

A crucial element of building a support network is active participation in your community. Attend local events, festivals, or workshops to meet new people and stay connected to your surroundings. Religious or spiritual communities can also be a source of companionship and support, offering a sense of shared purpose and belonging. By being involved in your community, you create opportunities for lasting friendships and meaningful connections.

Maintaining relationships requires effort and consistency. Regular communication is key to keeping relationships strong. This can be through phone calls, video chats, or in-person meetings. Technology can be a valuable tool for staying in touch with loved ones, especially if they live far away. Social media platforms, messaging apps, and virtual gatherings make it easier to maintain relationships even across distances.

For many retirees, loneliness can become a challenge. Being proactive about combating isolation is vital. If you find yourself feeling lonely, consider reaching out to old friends or joining social groups. Local senior centers often offer programs and activities designed to foster connections. These spaces provide a welcoming environment where you can engage with others and form new friendships.

A support network is not just about socializing; it's also about having people to rely on during challenging times. Identify individuals who can provide emotional, practical, or financial support when needed. This could include family members, trusted friends, or even professional advisors like financial planners or therapists. Having a dependable network ensures you're not navigating difficulties alone.

Mentorship can also play a role in building connections. Sharing your experiences and skills with younger individuals creates meaningful relationships and provides a sense of purpose. Whether through formal mentoring programs or informal relationships, guiding others can be rewarding and fulfilling.

Creating a support network isn't limited to people you already know. Stepping outside your comfort zone and initiating conversations with strangers can lead to surprising and valuable connections. Smile, introduce yourself, and show genuine interest in others. Building rapport takes time, but these small efforts can result in significant friendships.

Retirement can also be a time to reconnect with old friends or family members you may have lost touch with. Reflect on people who were once important in your life and consider reaching out. A simple message or phone call can rekindle bonds and provide a sense of nostalgia and continuity in your life.

Fostering social connections should also include self-care. Relationships are most fulfilling when both parties are happy and healthy. Take care of your emotional and physical well-being to ensure you're in a position to contribute positively to your relationships. This might involve setting boundaries, managing stress, and addressing any unresolved conflicts.

Prioritize quality over quantity when it comes to relationships. It's better to have a few meaningful connections than numerous superficial ones. Invest time and energy into relationships that bring joy, support, and mutual respect. These connections are the foundation of a strong support network and can make your retirement years truly enriching.

Building a support network and maintaining social connections is an ongoing process that requires time, effort, and intention. By focusing on relationships that uplift and inspire you, you can create a safety net of companionship and support that enhances your overall quality of life during retirement.

Embracing Volunteerism and Community Engagement

Volunteering and community engagement offer invaluable opportunities for single women in retirement to lead purposeful, fulfilling lives while contributing positively to society. This phase of life provides a unique chance to explore new interests, share valuable skills, and connect with others, all of which enrich your retirement years. By dedicating your time and energy to causes you care about, you not only improve the lives of others but also experience a deeper sense of satisfaction, belonging, and personal growth.

Volunteering allows you to align your passions with meaningful activities. Whether your interests lie in education, environmental conservation, healthcare, or the arts, there is a wide array of organizations and initiatives that would benefit from your skills and enthusiasm. For instance, if you have a passion for teaching, you might consider tutoring children, mentoring young professionals, or assisting adult literacy programs. For nature lovers, participating in local cleanup projects or tree-planting initiatives can offer both physical activity and a sense of accomplishment.

One significant advantage of volunteering is the opportunity to stay socially connected. Retirement can sometimes lead to feelings of isolation, but being part of a community project helps combat loneliness by fostering a sense of camaraderie and shared purpose. Volunteering puts you in touch with like-minded individuals who share your values and interests, creating meaningful relationships that may evolve into lasting friendships.

Community engagement also allows retirees to stay mentally and physically active. Many volunteer roles involve problem-solving, planning, and teamwork, which keep your mind sharp. Similarly, activities like working at food banks, participating in building projects, or engaging in outdoor conservation efforts promote physical well-being. Staying active in these ways contributes to overall health and vitality during retirement.

Another important aspect of volunteering is the chance to make a tangible impact. Retirement gives you the time and freedom to invest deeply in causes that matter to you. By volunteering regularly, you can witness the direct results of your efforts, whether it's a child's improved grades, a cleaner neighborhood park, or an organization's enhanced capacity to serve its community. These visible outcomes provide a profound sense of accomplishment and purpose.

Engaging in community service also presents opportunities to learn and grow. Volunteering often involves acquiring new skills, from public speaking and event coordination to technical know-how and interpersonal communication. These skills not only enhance your effectiveness as a volunteer but also contribute to your personal development and confidence.

For retirees seeking flexible commitments, volunteering offers a variety of options. Some roles require only a few hours a month, while others may involve more regular participation. Many organizations also provide remote or virtual opportunities, enabling you to contribute from the comfort of your home. For example, nonprofits often seek volunteers to manage social media accounts, write grant proposals, or provide online mentorship.

Community engagement extends beyond formal volunteering roles. Participating in local events, joining neighborhood associations, or organizing community drives are other ways to stay involved. These activities not only strengthen community ties but also offer chances to celebrate shared achievements and cultural heritage.

Volunteering can also be a way to bridge generational gaps and share wisdom. Many organizations, such as schools, youth clubs, or mentorship programs, value the experience and guidance older adults bring. By working with younger generations, you can impart life lessons, share professional expertise, and help shape the leaders of tomorrow.

In addition to benefiting others, volunteering can improve your emotional well-being. Studies have shown that helping others can reduce stress, combat depression, and increase overall happiness. Knowing that your time and efforts are making a difference provides a sense of fulfillment and enhances your sense of identity and self-worth.

Financial limitations during retirement do not prevent meaningful contributions to your community. Volunteering doesn't require monetary resources, only your time, dedication, and willingness to make a difference. Moreover, many volunteer organizations provide resources, training, and support to ensure you can participate effectively.

Retirees interested in exploring volunteer opportunities should start by researching local organizations or causes that resonate with their values. Libraries, community centers, and online platforms often list volunteer openings. Attending local events or networking with community leaders can also uncover opportunities to get involved. It's important to choose roles that match your interests, skills, and availability to ensure a rewarding experience.

Embracing volunteerism and community engagement enriches not only your life but also the lives of those you serve. By dedicating your time and talents to meaningful causes, you create a legacy of kindness and support that inspires others to do the same. This mutual exchange of giving and receiving fosters a vibrant and connected community, making retirement a time of renewal, purpose, and joy.

CHAPTER 7

Managing Risks and Safeguarding Your Future

Understanding Estate Planning and Wills

Estate planning is an essential process for safeguarding your assets and ensuring that your wishes are honored after your passing. It's especially critical for single women, as they may not have a spouse to handle these matters. Understanding the basics of estate planning, including wills, trusts, and beneficiaries, is the first step toward securing your financial future and providing peace of mind for yourself and your loved ones.

A will is one of the most fundamental documents in estate planning. It allows you to specify how your property and assets will be distributed upon your death. In your will, you can designate beneficiaries who will inherit specific items or financial resources. Without a will, the distribution of your estate will be determined by state laws, which may not align with your wishes. For instance, distant relatives may receive your assets even if you intended them for close friends or charitable organizations. Creating a will ensures that your desires are clearly documented and legally enforceable.

In addition to specifying beneficiaries, a will allows you to name an executor. This person is responsible for carrying out the instructions in your will, including settling debts, managing taxes, and distributing assets. Choosing someone trustworthy and capable to serve as your executor is crucial, as they will play a pivotal role in ensuring that your estate is handled smoothly and efficiently.

While a will covers many aspects of estate planning, certain assets may bypass it entirely. These include accounts or properties with designated beneficiaries, such as life insurance policies, retirement accounts, or payable-on-death bank accounts. It's vital to regularly review and update these beneficiary designations to ensure they align with your current intentions. For example, if you originally listed a family member as a beneficiary but later wished to leave the funds to a charitable cause, you'll need to make that change directly with the financial institution or policyholder.

Trusts are another key component of estate planning and offer additional flexibility and control over asset distribution. Unlike a will, a trust can go into effect while you're still alive. Trusts are particularly useful if you want to manage how and when your beneficiaries receive their inheritance. For instance, you could establish a trust that provides financial support to a loved one in installments rather than a lump sum. This approach is especially helpful for beneficiaries who may lack financial experience or discipline.

A trust can also help you avoid probate, a legal process where a court oversees the distribution of your estate. Probate can be time-consuming and costly, and the details of your estate may become part of the public record. Assets placed in a trust generally bypass probate, ensuring a more private and efficient transfer to your beneficiaries.

In addition to wills and trusts, estate planning involves addressing healthcare and financial decisions in case you become incapacitated. A durable power of attorney allows you to appoint someone to make financial decisions on your behalf if you're unable to do so. Similarly, a healthcare power of attorney designates a person to make medical decisions for you. These documents are vital for ensuring that your wishes are respected and your affairs are managed appropriately during unexpected situations.

Another important aspect of estate planning is planning for taxes. Depending on the size of your estate and state laws, taxes could significantly reduce the amount your beneficiaries receive. Working with a financial advisor or estate planning attorney can help you structure your estate to minimize tax liabilities. Strategies may include gifting assets during your lifetime or placing them in certain types of trusts that offer tax advantages.

For single women, estate planning also presents an opportunity to support causes you care deeply about. Charitable giving can be incorporated into your estate plan through bequests in your will or the establishment of a charitable trust. This ensures that part of your legacy contributes to the betterment of society and reflects your values.

Estate planning is not a one-time task; it requires periodic updates to reflect changes in your life circumstances, financial situation, and laws. Major life events, such as purchasing a new home, inheriting assets, or experiencing a significant change in family relationships, may necessitate revisions to your will, trusts, and other estate planning documents. Regular reviews ensure that your plan remains accurate and effective.

Creating an estate plan might seem overwhelming, but breaking it into manageable steps can make the process more approachable. Start by making an inventory of your assets, including real estate, bank accounts, investments, personal possessions, and insurance policies. Then, think about your goals for these assets: who you want to benefit, how they should be distributed, and whether any specific instructions should accompany the transfer.

Seeking professional guidance is often a wise investment. An estate planning attorney can help you navigate legal complexities and create documents that comply with your state's laws. Financial advisors can provide insights into tax implications and strategies to grow and protect your assets. Together, they can ensure that your plan is comprehensive and tailored to your unique needs.

Estate planning is more than just a financial exercise; it's a way to take care of your loved ones, protect your legacy, and maintain control over your future. By addressing these aspects thoughtfully and proactively, you create a roadmap that provides security, clarity, and peace of mind for yourself and those who matter most to you.

Protecting Against Scams and Financial Exploitation

As retirees enjoy their hard-earned years of relaxation and independence, they also become prime targets for scammers and financial exploitation. Criminals often view retirees as vulnerable due to their age, potential isolation, or less familiarity with modern technology. Protecting yourself against these threats starts with understanding the most common types of scams and taking proactive steps to safeguard your financial wellbeing.

One of the most frequent scams targeting retirees is the imposter scam. In this scheme, a scammer pretends to be someone you trust, such as a government official, family member, or a representative from your bank. They might claim there's a problem with your Social Security benefits, a supposed legal issue, or even a fabricated emergency involving a loved one. These scams often use urgency and fear to pressure you into sending money or providing personal information. To avoid falling victim, always verify claims independently. Hang up the phone or ignore the email, then contact the supposed organization or individual directly through official channels.

Another prevalent scam involves phishing attacks, where fraudsters use fake emails or text messages to trick you into sharing sensitive information, such as account passwords or Social Security numbers. These messages often appear to come from legitimate institutions and include links to counterfeit websites. To protect yourself, avoid clicking on links in unsolicited messages and never provide personal information online unless you're certain of the website's authenticity. Look for signs of a secure site, such as a URL starting with "https" and a padlock symbol in the browser.

Scammers also exploit retirees through investment fraud. These schemes promise high returns with little to no risk, appealing to individuals looking to grow their retirement savings. Examples include Ponzi schemes, where payouts to early investors come from money contributed by newer investors, and phony investment opportunities in real estate or cryptocurrencies. To protect yourself, be wary of investments that sound too good to be true.

Research thoroughly and consult a trusted financial advisor before making any significant financial decisions.

A growing threat is tech support scams, where fraudsters claim to be from well-known technology companies. They may contact you to say your computer has been infected with a virus or hacked, then demand payment to "fix" the problem. They might even ask for remote access to your computer, allowing them to steal sensitive data. If you receive such a call or email, don't panic. Real tech companies don't contact customers in this way. If you're unsure, reach out directly to your device manufacturer or a trusted tech support service.

Romance scams can be particularly devastating emotionally and financially. In these cases, scammers create fake online personas to establish romantic relationships with their victims. Once trust is built, they fabricate stories of financial hardship and request money. Protect yourself by being cautious when forming relationships online. Avoid sharing personal details too quickly and be wary of anyone who requests money or refuses to meet in person.

Fraudsters also target retirees with lottery and sweepstakes scams. They inform you that you've won a large sum of money or a valuable prize but must pay taxes or fees upfront to claim it. In reality, legitimate lotteries never require payment to receive winnings. If you're contacted about a prize, take the time to verify its legitimacy before taking any action.

Another common scheme involves medical scams. Fraudsters might offer fake health insurance plans, sell counterfeit medications, or pretend to represent Medicare to steal personal information. To avoid these scams, rely on trusted medical providers and pharmacies, and ensure your Medicare information is protected. Contact Medicare directly if you have concerns about a communication or offer.

Preventing financial exploitation also involves safeguarding against manipulative individuals in your personal life. Unfortunately, some cases of financial abuse come from family members, caregivers, or close acquaintances. Warning signs include unauthorized access to your financial accounts, unusual withdrawals, or pressure to change your will or other legal documents. Establishing boundaries and working with a trusted attorney or financial advisor can help protect your assets.

To enhance your security, consider implementing these practical steps. First, monitor your financial accounts regularly for unusual activity. Many banks offer text or email alerts to notify you of transactions. If you spot any suspicious charges, report them immediately. Second, shred documents containing sensitive information, such as bank statements or medical records, before disposing of them. Identity thieves can obtain valuable details from discarded paperwork.

Using strong, unique passwords for all your online accounts is another critical layer of defense. Avoid using easily guessed passwords like your birthdate or "password123." Instead, combine uppercase and lowercase letters, numbers, and special characters. Consider using a password manager to securely store and generate complex passwords.

Educating yourself about common scams is a powerful tool in protecting your financial security. Stay informed by reading updates from trusted organizations such as the Federal Trade Commission or AARP, which frequently publish warnings about new scams. Participating in workshops or webinars on financial safety can also empower you with knowledge and confidence.

If you suspect you've encountered a scam, report it immediately. Contact your local law enforcement agency, the FTC, or the fraud department of your bank. Reporting scams helps authorities track and stop criminal activity, potentially saving others from becoming victims. Even if you've already provided money or information, taking swift action can mitigate the damage and prevent further exploitation.

Building a strong support network is another way to protect yourself. Discuss financial decisions and suspicious communications with trusted friends, family, or advisors. Having a second opinion can help you identify red flags that you might overlook. Social connections also reduce the isolation that scammers often exploit to manipulate their victims.

Approach all financial and personal matters with skepticism and caution. Trust your instincts, if something feels off or too good to be true, it likely is. Remember, legitimate businesses and government agencies won't pressure you to act immediately or provide sensitive information.

Taking the time to verify and reflect on a situation can make all the difference in safeguarding your retirement years.

Planning for the Unexpected: Insurance and Contingency Plans

Preparing for unexpected events is an essential part of financial and personal security, especially in retirement. Life is unpredictable, and sudden challenges like health issues, natural disasters, or financial setbacks can arise without warning. The best way to handle these uncertainties is by developing a robust plan that includes proper insurance coverage and well-thought-out contingency measures. By doing so, you can ensure peace of mind and protect yourself from unnecessary financial and emotional stress.

Insurance serves as the backbone of any plan for managing unforeseen events. Health insurance, for instance, is critical to protecting against the high costs of medical care. For retirees, ensuring comprehensive coverage through programs like Medicare, Medicare Advantage plans, or supplemental insurance is vital. While Medicare covers many healthcare needs, it doesn't address everything, such as dental, vision, or long-term care. Exploring and investing in supplemental plans that fill these gaps can save you from out-of-pocket expenses that could quickly deplete your savings.

Long-term care insurance is another important aspect of planning. This type of coverage helps pay for services like assisted living, nursing home care, or in-home caregivers, which can become necessary as you age. The costs of long-term care can be overwhelming, often running into thousands of dollars per month. By investing in long-term care insurance early, you can lock in lower premiums and reduce the financial burden on yourself and your family in the future.

Homeowners or renters insurance is equally essential for protecting your living environment.

This coverage safeguards your home and belongings from unexpected events such as fires, theft, or natural disasters. In addition to basic coverage, consider policies that include protection against floods or earthquakes if you live in high-risk areas. Review your policy periodically to ensure your coverage reflects the current value of your home and possessions, avoiding gaps that could leave you vulnerable.

Life insurance is another critical component, particularly if you have dependents or wish to leave a financial legacy. Even in retirement, a life insurance policy can help cover funeral expenses, pay off debts, or provide financial support for loved ones. For single women, life insurance can also serve as a tool for estate planning, ensuring that your assets are distributed according to your wishes.

Disability insurance is often overlooked but is incredibly valuable, even in retirement. It provides income replacement if you're unable to work due to an illness or injury. While Social Security Disability Insurance may be available, private policies often offer more comprehensive coverage and faster access to benefits.

Beyond insurance, creating contingency plans is a crucial step in preparing for the unexpected. Start by building an emergency fund, which serves as a financial cushion for unforeseen expenses. Aim to save three to six months' worth of living expenses in a readily accessible account. This fund can be used for urgent needs such as car repairs, home maintenance, or medical bills, preventing you from dipping into retirement savings or accumulating debt.

Developing a solid financial plan also involves diversifying your investments to minimize risks. Having a mix of stocks, bonds, and other assets ensures that your portfolio can withstand market fluctuations. Diversification reduces the likelihood of significant losses and helps maintain steady growth, even in uncertain economic times. Work with a financial advisor to tailor your investment strategy to your risk tolerance and retirement goals.

Creating a legal framework for contingency planning is equally important. Estate planning documents such as wills, trusts, and powers of attorney ensure that your wishes are honored if you're unable to make decisions yourself. A power of attorney grants someone you trust the authority to manage your financial or healthcare decisions, providing clarity and avoiding conflicts during difficult times. Similarly, a living will outlines your preferences for medical treatment, offering guidance to your loved ones in case of a critical health event.

Another valuable strategy is to maintain a clear and organized record of your financial and legal information. This includes account numbers, insurance policies, medical records, and contact details for advisors or attorneys. Keeping this information in a secure, easily accessible location ensures that you or your loved ones can quickly retrieve it when needed.

Communication plays a key role in contingency planning. Share your plans with trusted family members or friends, ensuring they understand your preferences and can act accordingly in an emergency. If you don't have close family, consider naming a professional executor or financial advisor to oversee your affairs.

Preparing for natural disasters or emergencies is also essential. Having a disaster preparedness kit with essentials such as water, non-perishable food, medications, and important documents can make a significant difference during crises. Familiarize yourself with local emergency procedures and evacuation routes, and consider joining community preparedness programs to stay informed and connected.

Fraud and identity theft are additional risks that can disrupt your financial stability. Protect yourself by monitoring your credit reports regularly, using strong passwords for online accounts, and being cautious with personal information. Consider identity theft protection services for added security.

Maintaining your physical and mental health is a vital part of contingency planning. Good health reduces the likelihood of unexpected medical issues and helps you handle emergencies more effectively. Prioritize regular check-ups, a balanced diet, exercise, and stress management techniques to stay resilient in the face of challenges.

Planning for the unexpected might feel overwhelming, but taking it step by step makes the process manageable. Start by assessing your current risks, exploring insurance options, and building an emergency fund. Regularly review and update your plans to ensure they align with your changing needs and circumstances. With proper preparation, you can face life's uncertainties with confidence, knowing you have the tools to protect your future.

CHAPTER 8

Strategies for Longevity in Retirement

Stretching Your Retirement Savings

Maximizing the longevity of your retirement savings requires a thoughtful approach to spending and resource management. By carefully planning how you use your funds, you can ensure that your savings last throughout your retirement years while maintaining the quality of life you desire. This involves understanding your financial needs, prioritizing essential expenses, and making informed decisions about discretionary spending.

The first step in stretching your retirement savings is creating a realistic budget tailored to your retirement lifestyle. Begin by assessing your fixed expenses, such as housing, utilities, insurance, and healthcare costs. These are non-negotiable and must be prioritized. Once you have a clear picture of your fixed expenses, estimate your discretionary costs, which may include hobbies, travel, dining out, and entertainment. Keep these discretionary expenses in check by allocating a reasonable portion of your budget to them.

Tracking your expenses is another key strategy. Regularly reviewing your spending habits can help identify areas where you might be overspending. For example, subscriptions, memberships, or services you no longer use can often be canceled to free up funds. This simple step ensures that your money is directed toward what truly matters to you.

One of the most effective ways to stretch your savings is by adopting a frugal mindset without compromising your quality of life. This doesn't mean giving up on enjoyable activities but finding more cost-effective ways to pursue them. For instance, instead of dining out frequently, you can experiment with cooking at home. Similarly, traveling during off-peak seasons or choosing less expensive destinations can allow you to enjoy your retirement adventures without straining your finances.

Minimizing debt is crucial in preserving your retirement savings. High-interest debt, such as credit card balances or personal loans, can quickly erode your funds. Prioritize paying off these debts before retirement or as early as possible during retirement. Avoid taking on new debt unless absolutely necessary, as repayment obligations can create unnecessary financial stress.

Downsizing your living arrangements is another way to reduce expenses. If maintaining a large home becomes burdensome or costly, consider moving to a smaller, more manageable property. Downsizing can lower utility bills, maintenance costs, and property taxes, freeing up additional funds for other needs. For those open to relocating, moving to an area with a lower cost of living can also significantly extend your savings.

Taking advantage of discounts and benefits designed for retirees is a smart way to make your money go further. Many businesses and organizations offer senior discounts on goods, services, and activities. From discounted movie tickets to reduced rates on public transportation, these savings can add up over time. Additionally, look into government programs that provide assistance or subsidies for healthcare, housing, or other essential services.

Careful withdrawal planning is essential to ensure your savings last. Adopting a sustainable withdrawal rate, such as the widely recommended 4% rule, can help you avoid depleting your funds too quickly. This approach suggests withdrawing 4% of your retirement portfolio in the first year and adjusting for inflation in subsequent years. While this rule provides a general guideline, it's important to tailor your withdrawal strategy to your unique circumstances and financial goals.

Diversifying your income sources is another effective way to preserve your savings. While many retirees rely on Social Security benefits, consider supplementing this income with part-time work, freelancing, or rental income if your health and circumstances permit. Earning even a small amount can reduce the pressure on your retirement savings, allowing them to grow or last longer.

Investing strategically during retirement is another way to stretch your funds. While your portfolio should prioritize low-risk investments to protect your principal, maintaining some exposure to growth-oriented assets, such as stocks, can help your savings keep pace with inflation. Work with a financial advisor to design an investment strategy that balances growth and stability based on your risk tolerance and financial goals.

Healthcare costs can consume a significant portion of your retirement savings, so managing these expenses is vital. Take advantage of preventive care to reduce the likelihood of costly medical issues. Staying active, eating a healthy diet, and maintaining regular check-ups can help you avoid expensive treatments down the road. Additionally, consider using a Health Savings Account if you're eligible before retirement to cover healthcare expenses tax-free.

Tax efficiency is another important consideration. Being mindful of the tax implications of your withdrawals can help you save money. For instance, withdrawing from tax-deferred accounts like traditional IRAs or 401(k)s may increase your taxable income, while withdrawals from Roth IRAs are typically tax-free. Understanding how your withdrawals affect your tax bracket can help you make smarter decisions.

Inflation is a silent but significant factor that can erode the purchasing power of your savings over time. To combat this, regularly reassess your budget and adjust your spending to reflect changes in costs. Building an inflation buffer into your financial plan by maintaining investments with growth potential can also help offset rising expenses.

Unexpected expenses, such as home repairs or medical emergencies, can quickly drain your savings if you're unprepared. Having a separate emergency fund dedicated to such situations can prevent you from dipping into your long-term savings. Keep this fund in a liquid, easily accessible account to ensure it's available when needed.

Sharing expenses can be a creative and effective way to stretch your savings. For example, moving in with family members or sharing housing with other retirees can significantly reduce living costs. Collaborative arrangements, such as carpooling or sharing meal preparation with others, can also help minimize daily expenses.

Embracing a minimalist lifestyle is another approach to making your savings last. By focusing on experiences rather than material possessions, you can find fulfillment without overspending. Simplifying your life can also reduce stress and create a sense of freedom during retirement.

Regularly revisiting and adjusting your financial plan is essential to staying on track. As circumstances change, such as shifts in healthcare needs or unexpected windfalls, update your plan to reflect these changes. Staying proactive and flexible ensures that you're always making the most of your resources.

Stretching your retirement savings is about striking a balance between enjoying your life and being mindful of your finances. By planning carefully, spending wisely, and staying adaptable, you can ensure that your savings support you throughout your retirement years while allowing you to live the fulfilling and secure life you've envisioned.

Exploring Part-time Work or Freelancing in Retirement

Part-time work or freelancing during retirement offers numerous benefits that go beyond supplementing your income. It can provide a sense of purpose, mental stimulation, and a structured routine while allowing you to maintain financial independence. For many retirees, this approach bridges the gap between full-time work and complete retirement, offering a fulfilling balance of leisure and productivity.

Supplementing your income through part-time work or freelancing is one of the most significant advantages. While savings and Social Security benefits form the core of retirement income, additional earnings can help cover unexpected expenses, support hobbies, or allow for discretionary spending on activities like travel. This supplemental income reduces the pressure on your retirement savings, enabling them to last longer.

Engaging in work during retirement also contributes to maintaining mental sharpness and cognitive health. Many jobs or freelance opportunities require problem-solving, learning new skills, or engaging with others, all of which stimulate the brain. Studies suggest that staying mentally active can lower the risk of cognitive decline, making part-time work not just financially rewarding but also beneficial for overall well-being.

Social interaction is another key benefit of part-time work or freelancing. Retirement can sometimes feel isolating, especially if your social circle shrinks. A part-time job or freelancing projects provide opportunities to connect with colleagues, clients, or community members, fostering a sense of belonging and reducing feelings of loneliness. Whether you're working in a local shop, teaching, or collaborating with clients online, these interactions can significantly enhance your social life.

Flexibility is a hallmark of freelancing and many part-time roles. Unlike traditional full-time employment, these options often allow you to choose your working hours, adjust your workload, and even take breaks when needed. This flexibility enables retirees to balance work with personal priorities, such as spending time with family, traveling, or pursuing hobbies. Freelancing, in particular, offers the freedom to work from home or remotely, which is ideal for retirees who prefer a comfortable and adaptable work environment.

Part-time work or freelancing can also help retirees explore their passions or discover new interests. Retirement provides a unique opportunity to focus on what you truly enjoy. For example, if you've always loved writing, you could explore freelance content creation or copywriting. Similarly, if you're passionate about crafts, you might consider selling handmade items online. Turning hobbies into income-generating activities can make the experience both enjoyable and financially rewarding.

Freelancing platforms and local opportunities offer diverse ways to engage in work that aligns with your skills and interests. Platforms like Upwork, Fiverr, and Etsy cater to freelancers in fields ranging from graphic design and writing to handmade goods and consulting. Alternatively, local part-time opportunities such as working at a library, tutoring, or assisting with events can be equally fulfilling. The key is to match your skills and preferences with roles that feel meaningful and enjoyable.

Working part-time can also help maintain a sense of structure and purpose. For many retirees, transitioning from a full-time career to complete retirement can feel disorienting. A part-time job or freelancing project provides a daily or weekly routine, offering a sense of accomplishment and motivation. This structure can enhance emotional well-being and give retirees a reason to stay active and engaged.

Beyond immediate financial and personal benefits, part-time work or freelancing can also provide tax advantages. Earnings from these activities can allow you to delay withdrawals from retirement accounts, such as IRAs or 401(k)s, potentially reducing your tax liability. Additionally, freelancers may qualify for tax deductions related to their business expenses, such as home office costs, internet usage, or supplies, further improving their financial situation.

Networking opportunities often accompany part-time work or freelancing, which can open doors to new experiences and connections. Whether it's meeting new people in your industry or joining professional groups, these networks can lead to collaborations, learning opportunities, and even additional income streams. Networking keeps you connected to the world and helps you stay updated on trends and developments in your field of interest.

For those worried about physical demands, many part-time jobs and freelance roles can be tailored to your health and energy levels. For instance, online tutoring, consulting, or writing requires minimal physical effort while still offering substantial engagement and income. If mobility or energy is a concern, look for roles that prioritize comfort and align with your capabilities.

Pursuing part-time work or freelancing during retirement also encourages continuous learning. Taking on new challenges, adapting to different technologies, or acquiring new skills keeps you intellectually engaged. For example, learning how to use freelance platforms or gaining expertise in social media management can enhance your employability while enriching your personal growth.

Carefully considering the type of work or freelancing that suits your lifestyle and financial goals is crucial. Start by evaluating your skills, interests, and availability. Ask yourself questions like: Do I want to work from home, or do I enjoy interacting with others in person? How many hours a week am I willing to dedicate to work? These reflections can guide your decisions and help you find opportunities that align with your values and priorities.

Balancing work and relaxation is important to ensure you don't feel overwhelmed during retirement. While additional income is valuable, remember that retirement is also about enjoying life. Set clear boundaries for your working hours and prioritize activities that bring you joy and relaxation. This balance will help you reap the benefits of part-time work or freelancing without compromising your well-being.

Building a professional reputation is essential for successful freelancing. Delivering high-quality work, meeting deadlines, and maintaining positive communication with clients can lead to repeat business and referrals. Over time, a strong reputation can allow you to charge competitive rates, further enhancing your financial benefits.

Part-time work or freelancing can provide a sense of financial security and peace of mind. Knowing that you have an additional income stream can alleviate worries about rising costs, unexpected expenses, or outliving your savings. This confidence can make retirement a more enjoyable and stress-free phase of life.

Engaging in part-time work or freelancing during retirement offers a blend of financial, personal, and emotional rewards. It enables you to stay connected, active, and financially secure while exploring your passions and maintaining your independence. By choosing roles that align with your skills and interests, you can create a fulfilling and balanced retirement experience.

Adjusting Your Financial Plan Over Time

Adjusting your financial plan over time is an essential aspect of maintaining stability and ensuring that your retirement years are as comfortable as possible. Financial plans are not static documents, they should evolve as your circumstances, needs, and priorities change. Regularly reviewing and making necessary adjustments to your plan ensures it remains relevant and effective in addressing your financial goals throughout retirement.

Begin by recognizing that your expenses in retirement may shift significantly over time. During the early years of retirement, you may spend more on travel, hobbies, or dining out as you enjoy your newfound freedom. As you age, healthcare and long-term care costs may take up a larger portion of your budget. Periodically assessing your spending patterns allows you to identify areas where adjustments are needed, ensuring you allocate your resources effectively.

Inflation is another factor that can impact your financial plan. Over the years, the cost of goods and services tends to rise, which can erode the purchasing power of your retirement income. Reviewing your plan annually or biannually allows you to account for inflation and explore strategies such as adjusting your withdrawal rates, investing in inflation-protected assets, or finding ways to minimize discretionary spending.

Life events and unexpected changes also necessitate adjustments to your financial plan. For example, changes in your health, the loss of a loved one, or a significant economic downturn may alter your financial needs or resources. Regular reviews ensure that your plan reflects your current reality and helps you navigate these challenges with minimal disruption.

Monitoring your investments is a critical part of keeping your financial plan up to date. Market conditions can fluctuate, affecting the value of your retirement portfolio. Periodic reviews help you assess whether your investment strategy is still aligned with your risk tolerance and long-term goals. If necessary, you can rebalance your portfolio to maintain the desired asset allocation, reducing risk as you age while ensuring steady growth.

Reviewing your retirement income sources is another important step. This includes Social Security benefits, pensions, annuities, and any income from part-time work or freelancing. Make sure these sources are performing as expected and consider exploring ways to maximize them. For instance, delaying Social Security benefits can result in larger monthly payments, while restructuring annuities might offer more favorable terms.

Tax planning is an area that often requires adjustments over time. Tax laws and regulations change, and your income sources may vary year by year. Working with a financial advisor or tax professional can help you identify tax-efficient strategies, such as timing withdrawals from tax-deferred accounts or utilizing Roth conversions to minimize your tax burden and preserve your wealth.

Healthcare costs are another critical consideration in retirement. As you age, medical expenses often increase, and unexpected health issues can significantly impact your budget. Reviewing your health insurance coverage, including Medicare or supplemental plans, ensures you have adequate protection while avoiding excessive costs. Additionally, setting aside funds in a health savings account or similar vehicle can help cover future medical expenses.

Tracking your withdrawal rates is essential to maintaining the longevity of your savings. Many financial advisors recommend following the 4% rule, which suggests withdrawing 4% of your portfolio annually, adjusted for inflation. However, this guideline may not suit everyone, particularly during periods of market volatility or if your expenses fluctuate. Adjusting your withdrawal rate to align with your current needs and market conditions helps ensure your funds last throughout your retirement.

Creating a contingency fund is another valuable strategy to protect against unforeseen events. Setting aside a portion of your savings for emergencies ensures that you're prepared for unexpected expenses, such as home repairs, major medical bills, or family support. Regularly evaluating the adequacy of this fund allows you to replenish it as needed.

Reviewing and updating your estate plan is also an integral part of managing your financial plan. Over time, your family structure, relationships, and assets may change. Regularly updating your will, trusts, and beneficiary designations ensures that your assets are distributed according to your wishes and helps minimize potential disputes among your heirs.

Periodic financial reviews also provide an opportunity to reflect on your personal goals and priorities. As you progress through retirement, your interests and aspirations may evolve. For example, you might decide to dedicate more resources to charitable giving, support grandchildren's education, or fund travel experiences. Adjusting your plan to accommodate these goals ensures your financial decisions align with what matters most to you.

Working with a financial advisor can make the process of adjusting your plan more effective. A professional can provide insights into market trends, tax strategies, and budgeting techniques, ensuring your plan remains optimized. They can also help you stay disciplined and avoid emotional decisions that could negatively impact your finances.

Technology can also assist in managing and adjusting your financial plan. Numerous budgeting and investment tools are available to help track your expenses, monitor your portfolio, and forecast your financial future. Using these tools regularly allows you to identify potential issues early and take corrective action promptly.

It's important to involve your family in the financial planning process, especially if they may be impacted by your decisions. Discussing your plan with trusted loved ones ensures they understand your goals and can provide support if needed. For example, sharing your plans for long-term care or estate distribution can prevent misunderstandings and foster collaboration.

Maintaining a proactive mindset is crucial when adjusting your financial plan. Retirement is a dynamic phase of life, and staying engaged with your finances ensures you're prepared to adapt to changes. Regular reviews, whether quarterly, semi-annually, or annually, help you stay on track and avoid surprises.

Adjusting your financial plan over time is an ongoing process that ensures you can enjoy a secure and fulfilling retirement. By reviewing your expenses, investments, income sources, and long-term goals regularly, you can respond effectively to changes in your circumstances. This adaptability not only safeguards your financial health but also provides peace of mind, allowing you to focus on enjoying the opportunities and experiences retirement offers.

CONCLUSION

Empowering Single Women to Take Charge of Their Retirement

Retirement represents a significant milestone in life, a time to enjoy the freedom, peace, and fulfillment that you've worked so hard to achieve. For single women, it is a particularly empowering opportunity to shape a future that aligns with personal dreams and values. Taking proactive steps today lays the foundation for a retirement that is not only financially secure but also deeply meaningful. This journey requires confidence, planning, and a commitment to making informed decisions about every aspect of your life.

The first step toward securing your ideal retirement is embracing your independence and recognizing the strength it brings. As a single woman, you have the unique advantage of designing a lifestyle centered entirely on your preferences, passions, and priorities. This is your chance to create a vision for retirement that reflects who you are and what truly matters to you. By taking charge of your financial planning, health, housing, and lifestyle goals, you become the architect of your future.

One of the most powerful ways to prepare for retirement is by cultivating financial literacy and taking control of your finances. Understanding budgeting, saving, and investing empowers you to make decisions that align with your long-term goals. It's never too early or too late to assess your retirement savings, create a realistic budget, and explore opportunities to grow your wealth. Every step you take toward building financial security strengthens your confidence and ensures a stable foundation for your later years.

In addition to financial planning, nurturing your physical and mental well-being is critical to enjoying a fulfilling retirement. Staying active, eating healthily, and prioritizing self-care can help you maintain vitality and energy as you age. Just as importantly, fostering positive mental health through stress management, hobbies, and meaningful relationships enhances your overall quality of life. Remember, retirement is not just about surviving, it's about thriving.

Community and social connections are also essential components of a joyful retirement. Building strong relationships with family, friends, and neighbors enriches your life and creates a support network you can rely on. Whether through volunteer work, community engagement, or simply spending quality time with loved ones, surrounding yourself with positive influences fosters happiness and a sense of belonging.

Planning for the unexpected is another vital aspect of securing your future. Life is unpredictable, but with proper insurance, contingency plans, and a clear estate strategy, you can safeguard yourself against unforeseen challenges. These measures ensure that you're prepared for any situation, providing peace of mind as you enjoy your retirement years.

Above all, remain adaptable and open to new possibilities. Life is full of changes, and retirement is no exception. Periodically revisiting your goals, reviewing your financial plan, and adjusting your priorities allows you to stay on track and make the most of this chapter. Embrace change as an opportunity for growth and exploration, rather than a source of stress or fear.

As you take these steps, remember that the key to a fulfilling retirement lies in self-confidence and proactive planning. Believe in your ability to create the life you envision, and take ownership of your journey. Every decision you make today brings you closer to a retirement that is not only secure but also filled with purpose and joy. You deserve to live your golden years with the freedom and satisfaction you've worked so hard to achieve.